KNOW HIM IN THE
BREAKING OF THE BREAD

KNOW HIM IN THE
BREAKING OF THE BREAD

A Guide to the Mass

by

Fr. Francis Randolph

IGNATIUS PRESS   SAN FRANCISCO

Original edition published in Great Britain
in 1994 by HarperCollins*Religious*
© 1994 Francis Randolph

Cover art: *Supper at Emmaus* (detail)
Vicenzo Catena
Coll. Contini-Bonacossi
Florence, Italy
Scala/Art Resource, New York

Cover design by Roxanne Mei Lum

Revised edition © 1998 Ignatius Press, San Francisco
ISBN 0-89870-701-3
Library of Congress catalogue number 98-72284
Printed in the United States of America

Contents

Preface to the American Edition

In the eighteen years since my ordination, I have been made increasingly aware that our greatest act of worship, the Holy Mass, still needs to be explained so that the faithful may be able to understand more and, through understanding, come to a greater love. Many Catholics are still confused, upset, or ignorant about why we celebrate Mass in the particular way we do. Many more, especially the young ones, are frankly bored. On inquiry, I find that young people have never heard anyone explain to them what the Mass is about, while older ones, who knew what the Mass was about in the old days, have never understood why it was changed or what the new elements in the Mass mean. What should be the central and unifying feature of our Christian life has become for many a source of division, for others a tedious and irrelevant ritual. When I see good, conscientious youngsters walking away from the Church repeating "the Mass is boring", I feel something should be done for them. And when I hear devout elderly people who attend Mass every day confess with tears in their eyes that they still feel terribly guilty about not liking the changes in the Mass, I feel that they too deserve a sympathetic hearing.

I have observed also, in the years of my priesthood, a steady and relentless fall in the numbers of those attending Mass in England, and I hear of the same decline in North America and other "developed" countries. I worked for many years in a prosperous part of England, where the population has increased continuously since World War II. I find from the published statistics in the diocesan yearbooks that from 1945 to 1965 the Mass attendance rose from 30,000 to 74,000 and that from 1965 it began to fall, until by 1995 it was less than 46,000. That I find disturbing, even bearing in mind that parish priests do tend to underestimate their Mass attendances. The drop began when the Mass was first changed: it did not begin with the celebrated encyclical *Humanae Vitae,* nor was it affected by such dramatic and expensive events as the 1980 National Pastoral Congress or the 1982 papal visit. People simply drifted away from the Mass, and they continue to drift away. When you ask them why, they reply either that "the Mass is boring" or that "it's not the same as it used to be."

The first remedy I tried, and it proved rather successful, was to explain to the people what it is that actually happens at Mass. I shall never forget my experience as a newly ordained deacon divulging to a group of sixteen-year-olds what the Eucharist means. They were fascinated, but they said "no one has ever said anything about this to us before." A few years later, as a university chaplain, my colleagues and I devoted a whole term's worth of Sunday sermons to going through the Mass point by point and explaining what it meant. The students loved it, and our Mass attendance increased noticeably. When I ran my own parish, I repeated the experiment, and again people expressed appreciation. More recently, during the Lent of 1992, I was supplying Mass at a small west country town, following the illness of the parish priest there, when the local diocese invited priests to preach about the Mass. Here again I found people appreciated a basic explanation of what is going on and what it means. The good people of that town may therefore recognize some of the pages that follow, as may the people of my little parish and some who were university students in 1983.

Other Considerations

In fairness I must point out that boredom and incomprehension are not the only reasons why people have stopped attending Mass. A significant reason, which many people cite, is that the Mass is so often badly celebrated, without care or reverence. Young people are quick to notice if the priest himself is bored with the Mass, rattles through it as if it were an unpleasant duty to be got over as soon as possible, or extends it into an entertainment entirely dominated by his own personality. A lot of teenagers and young people are fed up with being talked down to or enduring something like a school assembly, run by schoolteachers. There is not much I can do about that; I can have no influence on the way that other priests and parishes celebrate Mass. There are plenty of self-appointed liturgical experts only too ready to make suggestions; many of them are actually the cause of the flight from the churches. All I do is to try to celebrate Mass as well as I can, using the instructions provided by the Church and being sensitive to what I hear from the people. If there are hints in the pages that follow that parts of the Mass could be celebrated in ways different from what people are used to, that is only to use the flexibility written into the official instructions. I have tried or witnessed a number of such experiments within the Church's guidelines, and I know they can be useful in certain circumstances.

Another important, or rather crucial, point is that many people make no effort to integrate the rest of their lives with the Mass. They are Christians for three-quarters of an hour a week and pagans the rest of the time. No wonder the Mass seems out of touch with their everyday life! Resolving this last problem can only depend on the individual. I believe that if people rediscover the true meaning of the "lay apostolate", or the role of the laity in the modern Church, they will find that the Mass influences their daily life and becomes the focus and nourishment for a fully Christian vocation. But without daily prayer and a real attempt to live a Christian life at home, at work, and at play, the Mass will always be an uncomfortable embarrassment.

My aim in this book is to attempt to explain the Mass in such a way that people, whether young or not, will have some idea of what really is going on. This is not a technical work of scholarship, and I am not going to pad it out with long footnotes and bibliographies: there are plenty of technical books available already. Nor am I setting out to write a critique of recent liturgical fashions, though it would be dishonest to conceal my feelings about developments that I believe have caused distress to many ordinary people. Formal Church teaching is set out in the new *Catechism of the Catholic Church*, and you can check any doctrinal points there. Any matters of opinion are my own, and you can pay as little attention to them as you like.

The Incomprehensible Mass

There is a peculiar irony in facing up to the fact that so many people fail to understand the Mass, because, at a cost of millions, the Mass has only recently been translated from Latin into English. Surely now that it is in a modern language, anyone can understand what is going on. Lengthy explanations are not needed, for anyone can see and follow it. I shall say something later about the question of Latin in the Mass; for the moment it is enough to record that between 1964 and 1970, the words of the Mass (and the other ceremonies of the Church) were all translated from the Latin language in which they had been performed for nearly two thousand years into modern languages in virtually every country of the world. This caused a great deal of distress at the time, and the immediate drop in attendance that took place in the late 1960s was undoubtedly due to the fact that people felt uprooted, lost, strangers in a Church that had been their familiar home since childhood. But the steady falling away since then has another cause: it is lack of education.

This is easily proved by looking beyond the bounds of the Anglo-Saxon world. In other regions the decline in Mass attendance has not been at all so great. In Central Europe numbers have kept up reasonably well. In Eastern Europe the tearing of the Iron Curtain has revealed a Church that has increased in numbers and prestige during the years of darkness. In Africa and in Southeast Asia the growth has been dramatic. Great numbers of new converts are baptized into the Church year by year, and enthusiastic crowds gather for a Mass that really does look like a celebration. So the problem is not intrinsic to the Mass itself: it is more local.

I strongly suspect that the answer lies in the fact that many Catholic schools have had a declared policy of not actually teaching the children anything about the Catholic religion. We were clearly told by the directors of religious education that the school is not the place for "catechesis" or "religious instruction" and that it is not the job of the teacher to explain things to the children or to make them learn about the Mass. That, we were told, is the task of the parish and the home. The school provided religious *education*, meaning that it could help children to live their existing faith and deepen it, but it was not its task to instill that faith in the first place.[1] If parishes and parents have not been aware that it is up to them to explain the Mass to the children, now is the time to start. In other parts of the world the pattern is different; American readers will know their own situation, but I have noticed that when I hear a young American voice through the confessional grille, it is usually better informed and

[1] It is only fair to add that a few dioceses and some independent schools take a rather different view of the responsibilities of Catholic education.

more conscientious than its English contemporary, though it is not necessarily more successful at living up to its ideals! During the Communist era in Eastern Europe, everyone knew that schools did not teach religion, so parents and priests made sure it was done, often at considerable risks. In Africa and Asia, Catholic schools do take on the task of catechesis, and missions are also well equipped with trained catechists. Children are taught what the Mass is about, and so as they grow up they do have a chance to assimilate it and make it their own. Of course free will exists, and some will drift away in their teens whatever you do, but for that choice to be genuine, the young person must know what there is to accept or to reject.

When the Mass was in Latin, it was obvious that children needed to have it explained to them. Schools would take them through the text of the missal very carefully, telling them how to pronounce the words, explaining what every part of the Mass was about. While few could translate the Mass, all could understand it. The least-educated Catholic knew what was happening during the great actions of the Mass, the Offertory, the Consecration, Communion. Now we have a generation who know the words of the Mass but do not understand it. It is like a torrent of words endlessly poured out across the altar in a tedious lecture that somehow fails to wake its audience. Music and singing seem to be no more than decorations stuck on to make the main monologue less tiresome.

To arouse interest today, we must demonstrate the structure of the Mass, its different parts, changing and unchanging. We must show which parts are addressed to the congregation and which to God. We must reassure people that intellectual attention is not always required but that silent prayer is part of the Mass too. We must let the music appear integral to the Mass, not just an added entertainment. Above all we must recover the basic understanding of what the Mass is: the perpetual making present of the great action of our redemption.

Critical Mass

There is no point in shirking the issue that the present rite of Mass itself does raise problems, and there have been some interesting developments in tackling these problems during the last five years. Questions that could not be raised even ten years ago are now being discussed, and a spontaneous movement all over the world is giving voice to a demand for a *reform of the reform*.

The "reform" in question is of course that pushed through in the late 1960s. This followed the Second Vatican Council (1962–1965) and used its name, but it is now abundantly clear that the Council did not require or expect it. During this "reform", not only was the language changed, but the text was completely rewritten. This new text, promulgated in 1969 as the "New Order", or Missal, of Paul VI, was the work of a small committee of devotees led by Archbishop Annibale Bugnini. He wrote an account of how the new Mass was produced, *The Reform of the Liturgy, 1948–1975*,[2] which makes surprising reading, as it re - veals how many of the revisions were made despite opposition from the bishops and even from the Pope. It was characteristic of the reformers that they were totally convinced that they were always right and that contrary opinions were ill informed. Confusingly, this committee of reformers was known as the "consilium", which sounds almost the same as the Second Vatican Council, *concilium*, not to mention the radical theological journal *Concilium*. As a result, many people are convinced that the Second Vatican Council ordered changes that were actually the work of the committee or even of the journal. It was presented as a matter of moral obligation to approve of the "new Mass", as if it had been infallibly promulgated by an ecumenical council. In reality it is simply a matter of discipline to follow the instructions composed by the committee and promulgated on the sole authority of His Holiness Pope Paul VI.

The Council actually made very few suggestions for

[2] Collegeville, Minn.: Liturgical Press, 1990.

changes in the Mass, and certainly the bishops there present had no idea of replacing the existing rite altogether. Yet before the Council had met, the liturgical reformers had worked out and published their scheme for the new Mass.[3] The bishops, not all of whom were aware of the proposals of the liturgical group, contented themselves with general liturgical principles, which were equally applicable to the old Mass, and with making a very few specific recommendations, the most urgent of which was that the people be helped to understand the Mass more fully so that they could actually participate.[4] This instruction of the faithful is precisely what has been so badly missed.

The "new Mass" did not grow or develop organically out of the old but was a deliberate fresh start, in keeping with the mood of the 1950s and 1960s, which believed in the coming of a new era in human civilization and the necessary destruction of all previous cultural monuments. This is why His Eminence Cardinal Joseph Ratzinger has recently gone on record as considering the imposition of the new Mass to have been the most significant factor in the current crisis of authority in the worldwide Church.[5] Now, in the late

[3] See H. A. Reinhold, *Bringing the Mass to the People* (Baltimore, Md.: Helicon Press, 1960).

[4] Constitution on the Sacred Liturgy, *Sacrosanctum Concilium* [henceforth cited as SC], 18-19.

[5] See his autobiography, *From My Life: Memoirs, 1927–1977* (San Francisco: Ignatius Press, 1998).

1990s, we are seeing the weakness of the "modern-ist"approach. Town planners and architects are busily undoing the work of their predecessors; artists and musicians are rediscovering traditional forms; and in Liturgy, too, there has been a widespread return to older ways of presentation and performance. In the years I have been a priest, I have been finding the 1969 rite of Mass more and more unsatisfactory as an expres-sion of the faith of my people. Young people in particular have become more and more vocal in expressing their dissatisfaction. Those who do not walk away chanting "the Mass is boring" have gone out of their way to find Mass being celebrated in the old way and can become very forceful in their attacks on the new rite. Particular difficulties I observe are the fact that there are too many scriptural readings and that passages are often too obscure for an ordinary congre-gation. I also find the confrontation of priest against people across the altar distracting and feel that it throws too much emphasis on the person of the priest.

Among notable developments in the past few years has been the formation of Adoremus, the society for the Renewal of the Sacred Liturgy, dedicated to re-examining the changes in the Liturgy with regard to proposing a positive way forward. An important contribution to this has been Fr. Aidan Nichols' book *Looking at the Liturgy*.[6] Other similar initiatives have ap-

[6] San Francisco: Ignatius Press, 1996.

peared in different parts of the world. An international conference near Oxford in 1996 organized by the Centre for Faith and Culture looked at a wide range of liturgical issues under the title "Beyond the Prosaic" and issued a manifesto statement calling for a new liturgical movement to repair the damage.[7] Cardinal Ratzinger echoed this call in his memoirs cited above. At the same time in Europe a group of young people have formed "CIEL" (*Centre International des Études Liturgiques*) and organized a series of conferences at which the historic Liturgy of the Church is being examined and scholarship brought to bear on the meaning of the traditional Liturgy and how it can help the spiritual development of the present day.

The reaction from many bishops and pastors has on the whole been very negative. People who ask for the old Mass, or just for Mass with some dignity, may be ridiculed or ignored. The 1960s line is pushed as if it were the only possible one, and anyone who disagrees is condemned. May I mention the adventures of this little book of mine? Originally it was going to have an introduction by a friendly archbishop who had read the text and approved of it, making many helpful suggestions but agreeing with what I was saying. But then he sent it to the diocesan censor, who absolutely condemned it and refused permission for it to be published. That is why I have used a pseudonym, so as not

[7] Stratford Caldecott, ed., *Beyond the Prosaic* (Edinburgh, 1998).

to embarrass the archbishop! But I really do not believe I have said anything out of turn, especially given the present climate of helpful discussion. In the chapters that follow, I have not attempted to hide my unease about some aspects of the present rite of Mass, for nothing is gained by trying to deceive the public. At the same time I have increasingly come to realize that many features of the new Liturgy as normally found are not authentic either to the Council or to the instructions that go with the Missal. These, the *General Instruction of the Roman Missal* (cited as GIRM) are authoritative and can safely be followed as expressing the intentions of Pope Paul VI when he authorized the use of the new Missal in 1969. I believe a reformed Mass will come, although not in the near future: in the meantime, what we should do is to celebrate the Mass of Paul VI as carefully as possible and do our best to understand it and appreciate the underlying realities.

The English Translation of the Mass

Some complaints about the existing English text of the Mass are ill founded. First, it has not been widely understood that the majority of countries where Mass is celebrated in English are not actually English speaking; the text is intended also for those who speak

English as a second language and there may be some justification for its being less subtle than a native speaker would expect. Second, the text is in course of revision as I write, and a new translation of the English Missal is expected in a few years' time. By and large the samples I have seen are a great improvement on the 1970 edition, although there are going to be political problems over the divergent development of the language on opposite sides of the Atlantic. We may end up with more than one approved English text. Because of this state of flux in the translation, I have as far as possible avoided quoting passages of the existing translation in the chapters that follow. The structure of the Mass will not be affected by the new version, so to accompany this book you will need to provide yourself with the text in use in your church. Parts of the text may be available on a free leaflet, or you can buy a proper "missal", which will give you the full texts of the Mass including the readings.

The Eternal Mass

What is really important is not the temporary structure of the Mass, which has changed in the past and will certainly change again; what we celebrate is unchanging and eternal, the Sacrifice of the Mass itself. There are aspects of the present text that are unsatisfactory, just as there were aspects in the past that were unsatisfactory, but if we understand and realize what we are actually doing, the liturgical form pales into insignificance. Here in the Mass we meet our Lord Jesus Christ; we share in his birth, death, and Resurrection; we are nourished with his Body so that we may become the Mystical Body of Christ, which is the Church. Be aware of that, and whether the Mass is in the new rite or the old or another yet to come will not matter. I believe that there is nothing disloyal in sharing my hopes that a future revision of the Mass will repair some of the mistakes of the 1960s, but I also believe that in obedience to the established Church order it is my duty as a priest to celebrate the current rite of Mass as well as possible and to explain it to my people.

1

Know Him in the Breaking of Bread

The First Mass

In the evening of the first day of the week, two disciples were walking from Jerusalem to Emmaus. And one came up beside them and began to explain the Scriptures that told of Jesus the Christ, how he was destined to suffer and rise again. And as he spoke, the hearts of the disciples burned within them; they were stirred and enlightened by the new explanation of scriptural words they had heard so many times before. But it was not until they sat together, and he took bread and broke it, that they recognized that the person actually present with them was the same Jesus about whom they had been speaking (Lk 24:13–35).

From that day till this, Christians have met to hear the Scriptures explained and to know Jesus in the breaking of bread. These three elements are the essence of the Mass: Christians come together and discern the spirit of Jesus in each other. They listen to the Word of God, and their hearts burn within them as they hear it. And in the breaking of bread they recognize Jesus himself actually present, given for them.

The coming together is vital; it is only in the Church that the Mass can take place. This does not mean necessarily in a special church building, though that helps. Nor does it mean that many people are necessarily gathered on any particular occasion, though that is desirable. It means that the Mass is celebrated within the unity of the One Church, that the celebration is not a private, exclusive affair but is in conscious union with the Church throughout the world. One of the most moving descriptions of the Mass I have read is by the American Jesuit Walter Ciszek, who was a prisoner in the old Soviet Union. He managed to slip away into the forest with only one companion and celebrated Mass quietly and secretly, using a tree stump as an altar. And in so doing he was far from alone; he was one with millions of Catholics all over the world. The whole Church came into the heart of that forest; Christ was made present among a people who were unaware of his existence. That lonely Mass was very much the expression of Christians coming together, uniting in the one sacrifice.[1]

[1] Walter Ciszek, *He Leadeth Me* (San Francisco: Ignatius Press; 1995), 37.

Listening to the Word of God is vital; unless we have heard about Jesus, how can we love him? There may be only a brief, whispered passage from the Gospel, or there may be a long, drawn-out sequence of readings, but in one way or other the message of Scripture must be proclaimed. The Church first expressed her faith in the words of the Bible, and the long centuries of developing tradition have deepened and enhanced those words. We do not hear them alone but within the Church that gave birth to them, and even now, even after they have been spoken so many, many times, they are still capable of awakening our hearts to burn within us.

The breaking of bread is the apex of the Mass. In the Consecration of bread and wine and the sharing of that Blessed Sacrament among the faithful, we know Jesus himself, directly, without intermediary. Still it is within the Church alone that we find him, for the Church herself is actually constituted by the sharing of Holy Communion. It is in receiving the Body of Jesus Christ that we become his Body, the Universal Church. That is why St. Paul warns of the risks at stake if we try to partake of that Body without recognizing the Body, if we imagine that we can receive Communion without desiring to be part of that Body which is the Church (1 Cor 11:29). Jesus Christ is not a tame lion; we approach him at our peril if we defy him; but if we come in love, open to his Word, recognizing his

Body, then we shall be loved and welcomed indeed. We cannot impose conditions on him; we come to him to learn, to listen, to follow his guidance. And his message is always the same, the message of his love for us, his love for all our fellow creatures.

The Discipline of Secrecy

For some centuries after Pentecost, the Church remained very silent about the Mass. It was above all the "secret", the "mystery", the one thing known to initiated Christians that was on no account to be divulged to those outside the Church. Those preparing for baptism knew that some great secret was to come, but it was not revealed to them until after they had been baptized. The union between God and his people was too personal, too intimate to display in public to a cynical and unsympathetic world. As a result, our knowledge about early Christian worship has to be gleaned from hints and allusions, tantalizing comments like "the initiated will know what I am talking about", and ambiguous references that even now can puzzle the commentator. Paintings and graffiti in the catacombs help to fill out the picture, but it remains true that we do not really know what Liturgy in "the early Church" was like.

St. Justin Martyr

This makes it rather a surprise to find one author who tears the veil of secrecy. The martyr St. Justin, in about A.D. 150, wrote a book called the *Apologia,* which is a simple explanation of what Christians believe and what they do, intended to persuade the emperor and other hostile powers to let Christians live in peace. In the course of this *Apology*, he describes the Mass and explains briefly what it means. It had not yet come to its modern form, of course, but the basic elements are recognizable. The faithful meet on Sunday, and the "memoirs of the apostles" or the writings of the prophets are read for as long as time permits. Then the priest explains the readings and exhorts the people. They rise then and pray in common for themselves and for all men everywhere, so that they may be recognized to be good, loyal citizens. At the end of the prayers, they salute each other with a kiss. Then bread and a cup of water mixed with wine are brought to the priest; he offers them, giving thanks. All present give their assent in the word "Amen". Then the deacons distribute the Eucharist and carry it away to those who are absent. The congregation does not disperse before a collection has been taken.

As well as describing the actions of the Mass, St. Justin gives away the central secret of what it means: "We do not receive these things as if it were common bread and common drink, but just as Jesus Christ our Savior was made flesh through the Word of God, possessing flesh and blood to rescue us, in the same way the nourishment over which thanks have been given through the prayer of the Word who was with God, and which feeds our own body and blood as it is transformed, we have been taught to identify as the body and blood of that same Jesus who was made flesh." For this reason, he goes on to say, only those who are full members of the Church may receive the Eucharist. My own copy of Justin formerly belonged to a Protestant college, and someone has written in a neat eighteenth-century hand "Is not this a little like transubstantiation?" It is indeed: St. Justin in the second century is saying, in a slightly convoluted and undeveloped way, exactly what the Catholic Church has been teaching ever since. The basic structure of Justin's Mass is still recognizable: the coming together as members of one Church, the reading and explanation of Scripture, the prayer of the faithful, the sign of peace, and the offering and breaking of bread, which the faithful receive as the Body of Christ. The collection also is a familiar element![2]

After the conversion of the Empire, there was no

---

[2] Justin, *Apologia Prima*, 97–98; most accessible in Henry Bettenson, *Documents of the Christian Church* (London: Oxford Univ. Press, 1963), section VII, iv.

further need for secrecy in a world where everyone knew what the Christian faith was about. But now arose the opposite problem: since everyone knew the truth, there was no reason to write it down! As a result, systematic writings about the Mass are not found until it first came to be doubted, many centuries later. It is the great mediæval theologians, particularly St. Thomas, who first explored the meaning of the Mass in depth, not because the ideas were new in their time, but because it was only in their time that anyone had begun to question them.

Now that we again live in a pagan society that is hostile to the Church, like that of the ancient Roman Empire, it might seem a good idea to practice the discipline of secrecy again, but since the secret has been so widely published for so long it would be absurd to try to conceal it. All the same I often feel uneasy about the way in which the Mass is televised, filming the actual Consecration and the moment of Communion, as if the cameras were intruding on something too intimate for the public gaze. I am hoping at least that readers of this book will be sympathetic, will be trying to come to love our Lord, if they are not yet fully communicating members of his Catholic Church. In explaining what we mean when we talk of the presence of Jesus Christ, of transubstantiation, of the mystical union of Holy Communion, I am aware that I am treading on very delicate ground. I hope and trust that I am keeping firmly within the mainline tradition of the Church, to whose judgment everything I say is submitted.

2

Meeting Jesus in the Church

Holy Things and Holy Places

The heart of our faith is the belief that the Word became flesh, that God became part of his creation, in a particular place and time. Our faith is *incarnational*, that is to say, Christianity is not a purely spiritual religion, concerned only with ideas and abstractions, but is down to earth, solid, rooted in this material creation. That is why we believe that material things, physical bodies, actual places and buildings, can belong to God and can be made holy. In this the Church is at one with our Jewish predecessors; we set aside certain places, certain buildings, and certain objects, dedicated for the worship of God. They are kept for this purpose and for no other and are treated with love and respect for that reason. It is like the way we treat things that have belonged to someone we love very deeply, things they might have given us. We treasure them not for their cost or usefulness so much as because they are tokens of the love we have for their donor. Even when they are worn out, we dispose of them more carefully than we would otherwise. In the same way Catholics treat church buildings and furnishings with love because they belong to Jesus Christ, the Word made flesh, the lover of my soul.

The Church Building

A church is built and set aside for the worship of God, to be a place where Mass is celebrated, where the sacraments are administered, and where people can come at all times to pray, to be still in the presence of Jesus in the tabernacle. All through history Christians have delighted to give of their best to make God's house beautiful, to furnish it well, to make it a place where rich and poor alike can enjoy the very best that our hands can offer.

In most countries churches are delightful to visit and by their very artistic interest draw millions to enter them, first in curiosity, then in wonder, finally as often as not in prayer. In Britain and the United States, however, we are not usually so fortunate. Catholic churches in our countries are not on the whole master-pieces of architecture, and their furnishings are usually less than great religious art, so that often we have to worship despite the building, not because of it. There is not usually much we can do about an ugly church badly arranged unless we are prepared to contribute large sums of money, so we must compose ourselves to pray as best we may. Of course there are some churches that are quite uplifting in their own right, more often found in the traditional Catholic areas, and it is possible to work wonders on a bad building with a little love. I was once called in to celebrate Mass in one of the most notorious housing estates in England. It took me some time to identify the church; a bleak concrete block with no external sign whatever that it was a place of worship, just square brutal walls and reinforced plate glass. But inside, what a contrast! The little congregation had lavished time and attention on the building; they had polished the benches, scrubbed the floor, and starched the linen, watered and tended the potted plants (which gave it a rather Scandinavian appearance) until everything told of the care and affection the people had for their church. Here was a most unpromising building simply and cheaply transformed by a loving congregation into a church where it was easy to pray. So you need never despair of even the most austere 1960s concrete bunker! (Two years later I went back and found that they had put a tiled pitched roof on the church and built a little round tower with a cross on it, so that it shows up as a sign of hope in that dismal area.)

The Arrangement of a Church

Whatever the style and type of building, certain things will be found in every Catholic church, though not necessarily in the same relative positions. Formerly there was a standard arrangement, which was the same in all churches and is still found in many countries. The focus and heart of every church is the *tabernacle*, the strong safe in which to keep the Blessed Sacrament consecrated at Mass. It is veiled with a cover of the appropriate color, signaled by an ever-burning light, and placed prominently and centrally on the main axis of the church so that all who enter may acknowledge the presence of Jesus Christ among his people. Above and behind the tabernacle stands a *crucifix*, the symbol of how Jesus gives himself totally in his love for us. Immediately in front of the tabernacle is the *altar*, the great stone slab on which the sacrifice is offered. To one side is the pulpit or reading desk, to the other side the priest's chair. All these (except sometimes the pulpit) are enclosed in an area at the east end of the church, raised up and railed around and called the *sanctuary*. At some distance from the sanctuary, in a place prominent in its own right, is the *baptistery* containing the *font*, the stone basin in which children and adult converts are baptized. Near every door is found a smaller basin, or *stoup*, containing holy water. In every Catholic church there should be a statue or picture of our Lady, and usually of some other saint, to remind us of those who have gone before us in the love of God.

A more recent arrangement has found favor in many churches, particularly in England, owing to a misunderstanding of certain liturgical writers. The tabernacle, instead of being on the main axis and thus hidden behind the priest during Mass, is moved to one side to what in theory is a "place of honour, easily recognised by people entering the church and accessible from the sanctuary".[1] In the position formerly occupied by the tabernacle behind the altar, which has been positioned nearer the people, is a throne for the priest. The sanctuary area is usually opened up and lowered and often extended forward so that the altar is central to the building. The *General Instruction*, while recommending that "local custom" be respected, suggests that the Holy Eucharist could be reserved in "a chapel suited to the Faithful's private adoration and

---

[1] Bishops' Conference of England and Wales, *The Parish Church* (London: Catholic Truth Society, 1984), 25.

prayer",[2] which is appropriate in a church that is often crowded with tourists. However the position of the tabernacle should be prominent enough that all who enter the church may see at once where it is and be able to greet the Lord. Not all churches have been rearranged in accordance with the *Instruction*, and it is common to find the font in the sanctuary rather than in the recommended baptistery.[3] More seriously, the Blessed Sacrament has often been removed from sight altogether and hidden in an obscure corner, which is directly contrary to the letter and spirit of the Council documents. Statues and crucifixes are not as numerous, and a plain cross may be the only symbol, in accordance with a desire for ascetic simplicity.

On Entering the Church

When we enter the church, we first remind ourselves of our baptism by dipping our hand in the stoup of holy water and tracing a cross over ourselves in the name of the Father and of the Son and of the Holy Spirit. It is always a good idea to take time to pray in front of the tabernacle, wherever it is, before settling into our place for Mass. The normal gesture of reverence for the Lord in the tabernacle is to *genuflect*,

[2] GIRM 276.

[3] Bishops' Conference, *Parish Church,* 27.

bending the right knee until it touches the ground. We do this on entering and leaving the church and whenever passing in front of the tabernacle. If there is no tabernacle on the main axis of the church, we bow to the altar (not to the priest). It will take most people ten minutes or so to collect their thoughts and settle down after the hustle of traveling to church, so we should never aim at arriving at the church less than ten minutes before Mass starts—and we should allow more time if possible. (The great exception is if you have small children in tow—it is pretty heroic of you to get to Mass at all, and for your own peace of mind as well as other people's, it is probably best not to bring restless little ones in until just before Mass starts! But do try to get them near the front where they can see what is happening, or they will be even more restless.)

We prepare for Mass first by simply kneeling or sitting calmly, breathing steadily, and letting the turmoil, noise, and confusion of the street outside flow away from us, being still and at peace in God's presence. Now we look again at the texts coming up for today's Mass, read over the Gospel, and make sure we know what hymnbooks or sheets we shall need so that we do not have to get flustered again when Mass starts. If the church has statues or paintings that can help us to pray, we should look at them; if not, it might be better to keep our eyes shut. If the organist is playing a voluntary, we should just let our souls rise and fall with the melody, drifting toward the idea of God. There will be plenty of opportunity for vocal prayer or intense intellectual mental prayer later on; this moment before Mass is almost the only time the Church allows us for the prayer of quiet.

Vestments

Meanwhile, out of sight in the *sacristy*, things are being prepared for Mass. The priest will be putting on his *vestments*, the special clothes that take him out of himself and mark him as the servant of Christ and his Church. Again this is something we have preserved in continuity with our Old Testament ancestors; the sacred ministers are vested in solemn ceremonial robes, derived from garments of centuries ago. There are many reasons. One is to show us that the human sinful person is not important. In street dress the priest may be that uncouth boor who was so rude to your grandmother or that suave society man who is always having tea with the Duchess. I remember an old doctor who had been a prisoner of war telling me how he saw a priest arrive to say Mass dressed in Nazi military uniform with the eagle and hooked cross on his shoulders—but once he put on his vestments, the man ceased to matter; he became The Priest, the eternal ambassador between God and his people. Vestments are free from associations of class or wealth; they belong to the Church, not to the man. The splendor and elaboration with which Christians have loved to adorn vestments are not to decorate the man; rather, they tend to submerge him even more, drawing our attention to the timeless sacrifice, celebrated in similar vestments century after century all over the world.

That is not to say that there are not "fashions" in vestments as in everything else, and usually a set of vestments can be dated fairly accurately. In the 1960s they tended to be lightweight and very plain, of artificial fabric. In the 1980s came a fashion for very full, heavy, flowing robes, richly patterned. A more classical style is now preferred by many priests, the so-called "Roman", which is again light but of good quality fabric. The style really does not matter much, as long as the vestments are in keeping with the tradition of the Church.

The traditional vestments are seven, like so many other things in the Church. First comes the *cassock*, the long black gown that is really part of a priest's everyday dress. Next he wears the *amice*, a neck-cloth tied on with strings that keeps the other vestments clean. (Monks may wear this over the head like a hood, and it may have a decorated border that settles as a collar when the hood is put down.) When the priest puts on the amice, he is encouraged by a prayer for protection against the attacks of the devil. Then comes the *alb*, a floor-length white tunic with sleeves; it reminds us of the clean purity of the redeemed who follow the Lamb in the Apocalypse. The alb is held together with the *cincture*, a tasseled cord, which is accompanied by a prayer for chastity. The fourth vestment, not often seen these days, is the *maniple*, a strip of colored fabric worn over the left arm, which symbolizes the priest's readiness to endure suffering for the sake of Christ. Next is the *stole*, a long strip of the same colored fabric, worn around the neck. By origin it is actually the border of a Roman toga, which was worn colored by certain officials in the old Empire; it was a badge of rank and dignity and therefore survived when the cumbersome toga itself was abandoned. Because the toga was wrapped around and around, the stole was originally looped or crossed, though often now it is allowed to hang straight down. The prayer that goes with it speaks of the dignity that Christ has restored to us. Over all goes the *chasuble*, an oval of colored fabric with a hole for the head, rather like a Latin American poncho. It symbolizes charity, but the traditional prayer speaks of taking on the yoke of Christ so as to find grace.

The chasuble and stole (and maniple, if worn) make a set of the same fabric decorated in the same way. They may be in a variety of colors, four of which are in general use. White or gold celebrates joyful occasions such as Christmas, Easter, and the feasts of many saints. Red is for martyrs, the Passion, and for Pentecost. Violet is for somber occasions, Lent, Advent and penitential Masses. Ordinary days, with no special feast or season, are green. In addition in many countries black is used for funerals (although in England violet or white may be used.), and by a curious survival rose-pink appears for just two days of the year, the third Sunday of Advent and the fourth of Lent, as a let-up from the gloom of violet. In some areas other colors are authorized for use: blue is sometimes found for Masses in honor of our Lady.

If Mass is to be celebrated with some solemnity, there will be a deacon or two, who use the same vestments as far as the stole, but the latter is worn slung over the left shoulder. Instead of a chasuble, deacons wear a *dalmatic*, a loose tunic with short wide sleeves, which should match the priest's chasuble in color and fabric. A server may take the role of *subdeacon*, in which case he omits the stole, and his dalmatic is properly called a *tunicle*. Most servers wear the cassock and a cut-down version of the alb called a *cotta*, often fringed with lace, though in some churches they wear a version of the alb.

Requisites for Mass

While the priest is vesting, the sacristan will have prepared the various requisites for Mass. The altar will be covered with white cloths, and at least two candles will stand on it. Obviously these were originally to give light, but they also have a symbolic role. As the wax dissolves away giving light and heat, so we Christians surrender ourselves, giving up our own interests in order to become the light of the world.

Various books are needed for Mass: the principal one is the *Missal*, a large volume containing all the texts of the Mass except the readings; this will usually be placed on the altar. A smaller version may be provided for when the priest is at the chair. The Scripture readings are contained in the *Lectionary*, in which they are all set out conveniently for each day and occasion; this will be placed on the lectern or *ambo*. There may be a separate, more elaborately decorated book for the Gospel readings, carried in procession by the deacon. The intercessory prayers and parish notices may be written in books or on loose sheets of paper.

For the Sacrifice of the Mass, the most important utensils are the *chalice* and *paten*. The chalice is a cup, which should be of valuable metal and at least plated with gold inside. By far the most convenient form of chalice is one with a broad hollow foot and a thin stem connecting it to the cup, though many varieties have been produced. The paten is a concave metal plate, also gilded. In preparation for Mass, a *purificator*, a white linen cloth folded into a narrow strip, is normally draped over the chalice; the paten is placed on top, and a large *altar bread*, or *host*, placed on it. That is covered with a *pall*, a stiff square of white linen, and the whole is draped with a *veil*, usually of a color and fabric to match the chasuble. On top of this may be set a *burse*, also matching the chasuble, which is a square folder enclosing the *corporal*, a square of white linen folded into nine to fit into the burse.

For the people, a large number of small altar breads are prepared in a *ciborium*: this may take the form of a covered chalice, or it may be a flat, open bowl. Two extra chalices will be needed if Communion is to be given to the people in the form of wine. Wine and water are put into glass or metal jugs, or *cruets*, usually held on a little tray. In some parishes a small spoon is provided with the tray. There should also be a cruet of water and a little bowl for washing in, the *lavabo*, with a finger-towel of white linen. All of these are placed on a side table or *credence table*, near the altar. The chalice and paten may also be placed on the credence table, or they may be carried in by the priest.

The *altar breads* are made only of unleavened wheat flour and water and are the type of bread used by Jesus at the Last Supper. They are usually made by cloistered nuns and supplied in two sizes, the large one that the priest can break so that at least a few of the people can share in it and small ones for convenience in giving Communion to large numbers of people. Traditionally, altar breads are white, round, and thin—some parishes have experimented with thicker breads, and even wholemeal ones, though much of the biblical symbolism is lost if they are not white. The wine is simply pure wine made from grapes, supplied under guarantee that no chemicals have been added.

On great occasions, or at a solemn Mass, *incense* will be used. For this the *thurible* must be lit: it is a metal basin with a foot, suspended from chains, with a perforated metal cover that slides up and down on the chains. In it are placed two or three cakes of lit charcoal, on which goes a spoonful of incense, grains of solidified aromatic gums that burn on the charcoal and give off scented smoke. One server will carry the thurible, and another the incense container, which is shaped like a boat and is therefore called one. On this sort of occasion another server will be needed to carry a *processional cross* so that all enter the church led by the Cross of Jesus.

All these things are dedicated for God's service and are therefore treated with respect and cared for by the sacristans. Obviously Mass can be celebrated without most of them, for all that is absolutely necessary is a little wheaten bread and a few drops of wine.

Heroic priests have been able to celebrate Mass in Siberian prison camps using a crust salvaged from their rations and wine pressed from a handful of raisins, whispering the words from memory under cover of darkness. In emergency conditions God has always found a way to bring grace to his people. If we are not living in emergency conditions, one of the ways in which we can show our gratitude is by the care and love with which we prepare for Mass. If we are lucky enough to have a beautiful church and decent requisites for Mass, the least we can do is to keep them clean and in good condition. The Mass is the supreme expression of our love for God as well as of God's love for us: he gives us the best, and we can give our best in return. There is something remarkably mean in skimping on God's service, in economizing on love—rather as if a young man were to give his fiancée a plastic engagement ring. There was an extraordinary move a generation ago to make the Mass deliberately scruffy and disrespectful, as if we had no love to spare either for God or for his people. Mercifully that mood is now past, and priests and people everywhere are rediscovering how to make the Mass something beautiful for God.

3

Meeting Jesus in the People

The Congregation

If we cannot recognize Jesus in other people, we shall never recognize him in himself. When we worship him, we are not alone, for we come to him as part of his Church, and it is in the Church that he makes himself present on earth. Our private prayer, our private acts of Christian duty, our daily life wherever we may be, all find their meaning in the community of the Church. Circumstances may dictate that we are isolated and apparently alone at times, but if we are part of Christ's Church, we shall never be without the vast fellowship of all the saints joining in our prayer. A hermit may have the rare call to live alone, and even to celebrate Mass alone, but the true hermit follows that vocation for the sake of the whole Church, ever conscious of the community of the faithful for whom the prayers arise, on behalf of whom the Mass is offered. Mass is never a solitary activity, and whether we are the principal celebrant or are simply kneeling quietly behind a pillar, we are part of the community of Christ's faithful, the People of God, the Mystical Body of Christ, the Church.

The other people who gather with us to share in the Sacrifice of the Mass may present themselves to us in many different guises. Sometimes we attend Mass in our own parish, where most of the people are familiar to us, at least by sight. Sometimes we are in a vast pilgrimage church with a great throng, all in holiday mood. Sometimes we are in a small group each of whom knows the others intimately. Sometimes we are visitors, guests in a strange country, attending Mass in a language we cannot speak. Sometimes there may be no more than two of us, the priest and one server; sometimes there may be tens of thousands in a football stadium. And yet at every Mass the same thing happens: the sacrifice of Christ's Body and Blood is offered for the redemption of the world. We can never ignore other people when we come to Mass; we should not long for a private box, as if at the opera, or for a cosy circle of intimates excluding the stranger. The Mass is for all people.

It is always a temptation, of course, to form an inner circle, a closed group of those we feel at home with, and to confine our worship to the occasions when we can be together. Naturally it does happen that we feel a particular rapport with certain people, which can enhance our appreciation of the Mass, but such an experience should always lead us back to the wider community of the normal parish Mass. The experience of close rapport can come upon us unexpectedly. I always remember one occasion, soon after I was ordained, when I was staying in the Lake District with a group from our parish high school—a few teachers and a dozen or so pupils, all perfectly normal Catholic teenagers, in other words, not overly fond of attending Mass. We did celebrate Mass every day, but usually it was only the headmaster and a few others who attended. But one day we had started early to climb the highest peak in the district, descending in the afternoon to a little chapel, where I was to say Mass. We told the group that they were perfectly free to stay outside and fall asleep if they wanted to. I really did not expect many to come, and I did no "liturgical preparation" whatever, simply celebrating the straightforward Mass of the day with no frills. There was no singing; there were no novelties or adaptations. We were far too tired to do more than read out the Missal as it was printed. But they all did choose to come, and the atmosphere was strangely enhanced. All of them, perhaps especially the more out-of-touch teenagers, felt moved by the Mass, united, at one with God. They talked about it for months afterward. And about twelve years later, they turned up at my church for the child of one of them to be baptized, still remembering that occasion, still more or less in touch with each other and with the Church.

Now the point is that the experience of togetherness we felt after a week of being young together, climbing mountains together, drinking together in the evenings, could not have been artificially preserved by forming ourselves into a closed group that would always celebrate Mass together. What it did do was to stay with us as we came back into ordinary parish life. It convinced me that you do not "create community" by stylish variations in music and Liturgy. If the Mass is going to speak to the congregation, it will do so on its own merits, unadorned. Ornamentation and elaboration, music and grandeur may help, but they are no substitute for our simple, essential intention to join and meet our Lord.

When we attend Mass in an ordinary parish on a Sunday, which is our normal experience, we are part of a very mixed bag. There will be people of all ages, from the squalling infant to the dotty old lady. There may be university professors and mentally handicapped children. There will be people whose families have been in the area for many generations, and there will be the descendants of immigrants. There will be first-generation immigrants from Latin America, from East Africa or Goa, from Vietnam or from the troubled republics of Eastern Europe. There will be idle rich and industrious poor, company directors and beggars. In particular, there will be some who are "good Catholics", who attend Mass every Sunday and often on weekdays, who arrive early and follow the Mass with a missal, and there will be the "smoldering wicks", who slouch in halfway through, prop up the back wall, and never move their lips to answer a response. All of them belong in our Church, and all of them belong together. If we try to exclude anyone, we deny that the Church is really Catholic. We should never attempt to form a tightly closed "worshipping community" consisting only of the like-minded and the totally committed: our Mass is for all people.

When we arrive at Mass, we should be aware of the others. It may not always be appropriate or possible to greet them all outside the church, but we ought to be conscious of the fact that we belong together, to be on the lookout for the shy stranger or the perplexed foreigner, as well as having a smile and a nod for the difficult, the embarrassing, and the awkward. In choosing a place to sit, we should not just be motivated by the desire for privacy or the attraction of sitting next to the best-looking person in church; sometimes we may be needed to help a harassed mother with five babies and no visible husband, or someone in a wheelchair who will need to be helped up for Communion. In other words, when we come to Mass, we should want to be part of "this congregation here present" and should be prepared to accept the noisy and difficult ones as we have to accept them within our own families.

The Opening Rites

The Mass begins with ceremonies intended to bring the congregation together, to weld them into a single body, and to prepare them for the great actions that are to follow. A church full of individuals needs to be encouraged to pray together, and this is most easily done with music.

The *Introit*, or *entrance antiphon*, of the Mass sets the tone and states the theme of the celebration. Ideally the text is sung and accompanies the arrival of the priest and servers. In the past, the Introit was the first part of the Mass spoken or sung aloud, and so the first word of the Introit became the "title" or "name" of the Mass. For instance, the Introit for a Mass of the Dead began with the words "Requiem aeternam dona eis, Domine" (Eternal rest grant unto them, O Lord), and so Masses of the Dead are known as "Requiems" to this day. On the first Sunday after Easter, the Introit begins "Quasimodo gemini infantes" (like newborn children), and so in many countries what we call "Low Sunday" is called "Quasimodo Sunday".

The official Introit text is usually a single verse of

Scripture, which is supposed to be set to music and sung by the congregation or choir. One option is to use the Introit antiphon as a congregational response, while the choir sings other verses, for instance, from a psalm. In practice this is beyond most small parishes, so it has become customary to substitute a hymn that everyone can sing. Hymns at Mass bring their own peculiar problems, as tastes vary so widely, and choirmasters sometimes choose hymns without really taking into consideration what the occasion demands. The theme should be one of gathering and beginning, and there should be some relevance to the season, the feast, or occasion. When we join in the opening hymn, we are expressing our willingness to come together for Mass as well as our love and acceptance of the others around us (even if that woman next to us does sing flat and the man opposite is half a bar ahead). If we are listening to others who can sing better than we can, still the mood should be one of openness and community; we are all together, listening to this beautiful music (or tolerating this extraordinary composition), and that does give us a sense of unity in God's Church.

If Mass is not sung, the Introit is simply recited. In some parishes the whole congregation tries to recite it together, reading from a missalette, whereas in others it is spoken by a reader as the priest comes in, and in yet others the priest himself speaks it as he reaches the altar. In these cases it can be quite difficult to find much value in it; it appears rather abruptly and is over before we have time to find our place. It is not easily seen as a method of gathering the people and introducing the Mass.

During the Introit, then, the priest and servers arrive in the sanctuary. They genuflect to the Blessed Sacrament, and the priest goes up to the altar and kisses it. The Blessed Sacrament is Jesus himself, but the altar is a symbol or reminder of Christ, the Rock of Sacrifice. We feel instinctively that we want to kiss a photograph, a souvenir, a letter from someone we love—in the same way the priest can show his affection for his Lord by this ritual kiss on the altar. But the altar does not represent only Christ; it represents also the Church and the "prayers of the saints from under the altar", as described in the Apocalypse. It is for this reason that relics of saints are included in the altar, and the priest remembers them too when he reverences the altar. At a solemn Mass the priest honors the altar with incense, directing clouds of the scented smoke toward the altar by swinging the thurible.

The priest moves to the chair or lectern to begin the Mass. Facing the people, he greets them, beginning (as we begin all our prayers) with the sign of the cross. Three possible greetings are provided: the first is the long one that invokes all three Persons of the Trinity; the third is the short, traditional one: "The Lord be with you." This short greeting, with the people's answer, occurs several times during the Mass (though not as often as it used to) to build a close friendship between priest and people, a reassurance of their mutual goodwill. (The second option has been given two alternative responses, which makes it impossible for the people to know which one they are supposed to use, so this greeting has rather dropped out of use.)

The Rite of Penance

There follows the *Penitential Rite*. Many people are surprised that the Mass apparently begins on so negative a note, dwelling on past sins, and indeed originally this rite was positioned to prepare people to receive Communion. The Penitential Rite at the beginning of Mass was formerly a purely private affair among the ministers. When it was made public and emphasized as an introduction to the whole ceremony, the intention was to show that we should begin by breaking free of sin to be ready for the real action of the Mass. The priest introduces the rite, using one of three suggested formulae, or in his own words making reference to the occasion, the season, or the saint of the day. Priest and people reflect together on their sinful condition: none of us is fit to stand before God; we are all imperfect in one way or another; we may have some particular shame or problem. All of these points we bring into our prayer, and we reflect together on the love and forgiveness that God has guaranteed to give us as soon as we repent. Note that the priest is involved in this as well; he is not presiding over the people as they confess their sins, but joining them in confessing together. I once saw this dramatically expressed in a mission chapel in Zimbabwe, where at the invitation to confess their sins, priest and people fell on their knees together, all facing the same way, toward the altar, and all chanting the prayer of repentance to-gether. I have never dared do this in England, but it is important to emphasize that the priest is just as much a sinner as the rest, and like the rest is forgiven and saved by God's grace. (In the old Mass this was empha-sized by making the priest confess his sins to the people before they had a chance to confess their own!)

There are four forms of the Penitential Rite, which express this prayer of repentance and forgiveness. The first is a cut-down version of the *Confiteor*, an ancient prayer confessing not only to God but to one another and to all the angels and saints, asking the saints and each other to pray for forgiveness. The second, very short and not much used now, is a pair of invocations, each with a response, asking for mercy and love. The third is a revival of an ancient liturgical form, the *troped Kyrie*. Three pairs of invocation, "Lord have mercy, Christ have mercy, Lord have mercy", are interspersed with verses expressing faith in Jesus, an appreciation of his saving work, and our confidence in forgiveness. These verses, or "tropes", were originally sung during the long, drawn-out chanting of the words "Kyrie eleison" in the mediæval Mass. In the modern versions all refer to Jesus Christ, though formerly it was understood that the first and third pairs of invocations referred to the Father and Holy Spirit respectively. There are eight suggested sets of tropes in the Missal, some appropriate for particular seasons, others for general use.

A fourth option for the penitential rite is the *Asperges*, the blessing and sprinkling of water. We are baptized only once, but the Church positively encourages us to repeat the actions and promises of baptism as often as possible. A vessel of water is set before the priest, who invokes a blessing on it as a reminder of our baptism, asking God to renew the grace we received then. The priest and servers then process round the church, the priest sprinkling the water on the people, who make the rite their own with the sign of the cross. During this an appropriate chant may be sung.

At the end of the Penitential Rite, the priest sums up with a prayer invoking God's forgiveness and eternal life. Then after the first or second Penitential Rite comes the *Kyrie*, when the invocations "Lord have mercy, Christ have mercy, Lord have mercy" are each doubled. This is one of the Mass texts most often sung, and in the great musical settings it can be quite elaborate, with the invocations repeated over and over again. We now say each invocation twice, though always in the past in the Western rite each was said three times, and in the Eastern rite they are repeated endlessly, in one ceremony no less than five hundred times! We cry out for mercy as the blind beggar on the road to Jericho cried out over and over again, confident that the Lord would hear him. In all this the mood is subdued, sorrowful, ashamed, but growing in confidence. Like St. Peter, we fall on our knees before Jesus, saying "depart from me, O Lord, I am a sinful man", and we feel the Lord pulling us to our feet and assuring us of his love.

The Gloria

The mood changes dramatically as the Mass bursts into the *Gloria*, a hymn of thanks, praise, and triumph for the redemption we have received. It is very difficult at a said Mass to convey this change of mood; at the chapel I mentioned in Zimbabwe, they did it by jumping to their feet and breaking into joyful song with pounding drums and rattles. Careful selection of music should be able to produce the same effect elsewhere. The Gloria pours out a succession of scriptural snatches, prayers, acclamations, and praises of Jesus, who has taken on his shoulders the guilt of us all and set us free from our burdens, just as the scapegoat in the Old Testament was laden with the sins of the people and sent into the desert to carry them away. Because of the triumphalist joy of the Gloria, it is omitted completely when the whole Mass is of a penitential or simple character, in Advent and Lent and on ordinary weekdays.

The Collect

We have been assembled; we have been prepared; we have expressed our sorrow and our joy; and now we join the priest in the first great prayer of the Mass. He invites us to pray, and there is a silence during which each makes a silent prayer for the needs of the Church and the world. The priest then collects all these silent prayers in a brief *Opening Prayer*, formerly called a *Collect* for this reason. This is the first of what are called the "three prayers of the Mass" (we shall meet the other two later on). The Missal contains a very large number of sets of these three prayers, often with alternatives, drawn from a huge variety of sources. For certain days they are fixed, for instance, Christmas and Easter and the feasts of important saints. On other days, proper prayers are suggested, but others can be used; for instance, on any ordinary Sunday there is a suggested set, but those for any other ordinary Sunday may be substituted. On other occasions, for instance, Masses on special themes like peace or the spread of the gospel, there are several alternatives from which the priest may choose. All this can make it difficult for people who like to follow what is being said in their own missals.

The Opening Prayers all have the same structure, which does not come across very easily in English. They begin by calling on God the Father, recalling some point of our faith or some moment in salvation history, and then make a request in the name of Jesus Christ and in the unity of the Holy Spirit. The people make the prayer their own by responding "Amen". It is not always easy to follow these prayers, as the language can be quite convoluted, so we often have to make a general act of assent to "whatever that prayer was about". The prayer is not necessarily that of any individual; it is the prayer of the whole Church, and we can join in with the whole Church by our "Amen", even if we are not quite sure what has just been said. This is an important point that will need to be mentioned again: it is impossible for any normal person to follow, understand, appreciate, and take in every word of the Mass; we have to rely on the fact that it is a collective prayer, and at moments when our attention wanders someone else may be covering for us, just as when a huge chorus is singing together, an individual member can pause for breath from time to time without affecting the overall sound. If you cannot hear the Opening Prayer, and have not had time to find it in your missal before it is over, do not worry. Say the "Amen" with confidence, for you are joining in a huge chorus of prayer, with millions of people all over the world and throughout all time.

4

Meeting Jesus in the Word

The First Table

In *The Imitation of Christ,* Thomas à Kempis tells us that there are two tables at which we dine, that of the Word and that of the Sacrament. [1] Before we approach the Sacrifice and the Sacrament, we turn to the Scriptures, listening and learning, so that "our hearts may burn within us" and we may be prepared to "recognize Jesus in the breaking of bread". That is why the sequence of readings and instruction, the *Liturgy of the Word*, is an essential part of the Mass, the vital preparation without which we ought not to approach the altar of sacrifice. It is not optional, nor can we claim to have taken part in the Mass if we have missed the readings. To come deliberately too late for the readings and

[1] Thomas à Kempis, *The Imitation of Christ*, bk. 4, chap. 11.

sermon would be a gravely sinful insult to the Mass; to let the readings wash over us with no attempt to hear them would be to come unprepared to meet our Lord.

St. Jerome tells us that "ignorance of the Bible is ignorance of Christ." This does not of course mean that the Bible is our one and only source of information and faith; it is the living Catholic Church that not only wrote the Bible but continues to explain and develop its doctrines. Without the Church, we would have no Bible, and only the Church has the right to explain what she herself has written. That is why the Bible readings at Mass are followed by explanation and why difficult or ambiguous passages can safely be understood only if we remain within the tradition of the Church. When the Bible is left to be interpreted by every Christian in his own way, the result is an unbelievable number of quarreling sects all claiming to be "based on the Bible". The Catholic Church is not based on the Bible: the Bible comes to us on the authority of the Catholic Church.

The Lectionary

The description of the second-century Mass left to us by Justin says that the "memoirs of the Apostles [that is the Gospels] or the collections of the prophets are read for as long as possible", and at first the readings may well have been rather long and chosen for the occasion. It did not take the Church long to realize, however, that the attention span of a large, mixed congregation is fairly brief and that readings should be kept reasonably short. It must also have been apparent that if you leave it to the leaders of each congregation to choose their own readings, the people will be treated to a repetitive diet of the leaders' favorite passages. As a result there appeared the *Lectionary*, a book of selected passages from different parts of the Bible appointed to be read on specific days so that in the course of a year the people could hear all the most important texts and a good selection of the rest. Various different Lectionaries were in fact used, though the Roman version was in most common use for fifteen hundred years and formed the basis of many modern non-Catholic compilations as well. However, this original Roman version of the Lectionary was superceded in 1969, and a completely new Lectionary drawn up, which is the one we use today.

The modern Lectionary is arranged on a rather complicated pattern, with overlapping "cycles" of years. Basically, the *Sunday Lectionary* repeats itself on a three-year cycle, whereas the *Weekday Lectionary* works on a two-year cycle, both starting in 1969. To complicate matters, the readings for *Saints' Days* repeat, every year, and there are some Sundays and weekdays that are the same every year. What is more, there are many days on which there are alternative readings, and on most special occasions there is a wide range of choices. It can be very difficult to predict which readings will be used on any specific occasion.

The Sunday Readings

Let us begin with Sundays, for that is when most people experience Mass. The planners of the 1969 Lectionary decided to introduce three readings every Sunday, the first normally from the Old Testament, the second from the Epistles of the New Testament (mainly St. Paul) and the third from the Gospels. Between them were to be two responsorial psalms, the first with a varying antiphon and the second with Alleluias. All this adds up to an enormous bulk of Scripture, and fears were expressed when the proposals were unveiled in 1967 that it would be too much for most congregations. As a result, the Alleluia psalm was shortened, and the first responsorial psalm was made optional, as was one of the first two readings. In many European countries, as a result, the Liturgy of the Word consists of one reading, a short Alleluia response, and the Gospel. In England and the U.S., however, we nearly always use all three readings as well as the responsorial psalm. The congregation sits until the Alleluia verse, when it rises to greet the Gospel. One or two readers proclaim the readings, and the Gospel may be read by the priest or deacon, accompanied by candles and incense.

Preparing for Sunday Mass

All this Scripture has indeed proved to be too much for many people, and the result is that they struggle to understand the first reading, are frustrated by the psalm, baffled by St. Paul, and are asleep by the Gospel. Which is a pity, because the Gospel reading is naturally the most important as well as usually the easiest to follow. The solution, if the full-length Liturgy is being used, is to prepare for it in advance and to conserve your mental energy for the Gospel; that is, do not worry if you don't find very much spiritual nourishment in the first two readings. There are many inexpensive versions of the Missal on sale, and they are worth having, not so much to "follow the Mass" while it is actually going on, but to *prepare for it beforehand*. Preferably the night before, look up the readings for the coming Sunday, and begin by studying the Gospel. When you have an idea what that is about, look at the first reading and see if it echoes what you have seen in the Gospel (it is meant to). Then look at the psalm and see if you can make it your prayer, reflecting on what you have seen in the Gospel. Only then should you tackle the Epistle, look it up in your own Bible, and see if you can work out what St. Paul is saying. If you do this beforehand, then there is some chance that when you come to Mass you will get more out of the Liturgy of the Word. I really do not believe that anyone can make much of coming cold to the readings and sitting through them as they are performed in the average parish.

The Gospel Readings

We begin therefore with the Gospel, the story about what Jesus said and did. Every Christian must have at least some grasp of the Gospel story, but every one of us can find that no matter how many times we have read the Gospels, there is always something new to take us by surprise. There are certain days when the Gospel reading is directly relevant to the occasion being commemorated: on Easter Sunday we hear of the Resurrection, on Pentecost we hear Jesus promising to send the Holy Spirit. In certain seasons the Gospel readings are obviously appropriate: we have the stories of John the Baptist and the preparation for the birth of Jesus in Advent just before Christmas; we hear the story of Jesus fasting in the desert during Lent. The Sunday readings for the "seasons", that is to say, Advent and Christmastide, Lent and Eastertide, are all chosen with seasonal themes. In the process we have used up most of St. John's Gospel. That leaves just over half the year unaccounted for, the periods after Epiphany and after Pentecost, which are called "ordinary time". For these Sundays three sets of thirty-four weeks have been provided to be used as needed (if there are too many, one or two are lost during the Easter season). During these Sundays "of ordinary time" the Gospel of St. Matthew is read in Year A, that of St. Mark in Year B (filled out with more of St. John) and St. Luke in Year C. Fundamentally during each Year we begin after the story of the birth of Jesus and read the Gospel through in order, stopping before the beginning of the Passion narrative. One Sunday's Gospel reading is thus likely to be the passage immediately following the previous Sunday's.

It is characteristic of the Gospels that they come apart easily into short sections that can be understood on their own (technically called "pericopes"). The Gospel for any one Sunday is a complete story or a neat section of teaching that can be understood as a unit. The rest of the Bible was not written like that, and that is why the other readings can be much more difficult to understand unless you are familiar with the whole Bible. It is, I must say, an enormous advantage for any Christian to *be* familiar with the whole Bible, and systematic reading of the Bible, with the help of a Catholic commentary or notes, is tremendously worthwhile. If a chapter a day is read, it takes about four years to complete, and this will greatly enhance an understanding of the whole approach to Scripture. But in the meantime, we must do the best we can with the Lectionary.

The Old Testament Reading

Having looked at the Gospel reading for the coming Sunday, turn back to the first reading. Except in Eastertide (when we read the Acts of the Apostles, an easy narrative book), the first reading is an extract from one of the ancient Jewish books of the Old Testament. These readings are not normally easy to understand, particularly in Year C. But they are supposed to reflect the Gospel reading in some way. Sometimes the relevance is obvious, for instance, when the parable of the vineyard is matched to the song of the vineyard in Isaiah (Year A, Sunday 27), or the story of the feeding of the five thousand with five barley loaves to the similar story in Elisha's life (Year B, Sunday 17). Sometimes, however, the connection is rather obscure and, on occasion, can leave us baffled. It will probably help if you look up the Old Testament reading in your own Bible and read a little bit more on either side of the Sunday extract, particularly in the historical books. If you know who Elisha is and what he did in life, you will be more at home with the story of his miracle; if you read enough of Isaiah's poetry to have an idea of his message and the sort of times he lived in, you will see why Jesus told a parable that deliberately echoes Isaiah. St. Augustine said that the New Testament was hidden in the Old, and the Old Testament is explained by the New. It is fascinating to see how closely they are linked, how much of the Gospel revelation is already "foreshadowed" or reflected in the first revelation to the Jews, and how some of the more peculiar parts of the Old Testament take on a new meaning when we understand them as allegories about Christ and the Christian. We must remember that we are not saved by knowing about the history and archaeology of Palestine; we are saved by knowing Jesus Christ, and the value of the Old Testament is in what it tells us about him.

The Responsorial Psalms

I think most priests and people would agree that the weakest part of the new Liturgy is the "responsorial psalm". The experience in most churches is that the "response" is announced by a reader, who may or may not speak audibly, and the people are expected to chime in together whenever the reader stops. This means that the psalm verses have to be read at speed and all in one breath, otherwise people will start "responding" whenever the reader pauses for breath or effect. The poetry of the psalms is completely lost by this extraordinary treatment, and it can hardly be of any spiritual benefit to anyone.

To do justice to the liturgical planners, this is not what they intended. The method of inserting repeated antiphons between each verse of a psalm is quite effective when the psalm is sung. It seems that Père Gélineau was the first to write psalm settings of this type, and these settings, now forgotten, were very popular in the 1950s and 1960s. The idea is that a strong solo singer or a trained group of cantors introduces the antiphon, which is short enough for the whole congregation to sing again after them. The psalm can then be sung in unison or harmony by the expert singers, and the untrained people can satisfactorily repeat the antiphon at intervals, rather like the "chorus" of a folk song. We liked the Gélineau psalms when I was at school and sang them, even in the bus on the way back from an out-of-town game. They were effective as a way of introducing psalm-singing to boys who could never have tackled the complicated timing of plainsong.

When the Mass was revised, the idea was to use Gélineau psalms, or similar compositions, not just after the Old Testament reading but at five points in the Mass: the entrance procession, after both readings, at the Offertory and after Communion. When the plans were unveiled at the 1967 Synod, the bishops rebelled and insisted on reducing the number to the present one psalm, believing that in the majority of churches throughout the world singing would not be possible and that the psalm would have to be recited in the present dreary way. Now in reality, most parishes ought to be able to find a soloist or choir capable of leading the Sunday congregation in singing the psalm. As well as the old Gélineau settings, there are now several alternative resource books available, so that a valued part of the Liturgy could be restored. Failing that, nearly all psalms have been turned into metrical hymns that the whole congregation could sing together. If the psalm really cannot be sung, the *General Instruction* suggests either that the whole congregation recite it together (easy if all have missals or missalettes) or that a good reader, not the same one who is doing the readings, can read it uninterrupted as a meditation. Or, if there is only one reading before the Gospel, the psalm can be omitted altogether.[2] But if your parish still recites it in the usual manner, I do not think there is much to be done to salvage it for prayer—come back to it later as a private meditation. The psalm is chosen as far as possible to pick up themes explored in the Gospel and Old Testament reading, and in our

---

[2] GIRM 36–39.

private meditation we can look for this connecting theme or echo. Psalms are prayer-poems of amazing profundity, reflecting different moods and spiritual themes, and I find the original 1963 Grail version used in Britain very satisfactory in giving an impression of the Hebrew verse-structure and rhythm.

The Alleluia Verse

Immediately before the Gospel, the Alleluia verse is all that survives of the responsorial psalm rejected by the bishops in 1967. The joyful acclamation *Alleluia!* brackets a single verse of Scripture, which looks forward to the Gospel reading. It is meant to be rather triumphant and should be spoken or sung with some vigor—musical settings can be quite dramatic. Because it is so short, it can be effective as an acclamation when it is not sung, though it may be omitted. The idea is to draw attention to the importance of the coming Gospel.

Because Alleluia is a joyful resurrection-sort of shout, it has always been considered inappropriate during Lent. Another phrase such as "Glory to you, O Christ" is substituted, even on a major feast like St Joseph's day (March 19). The Alleluia is banished until the end of Lent, which makes its triumphant return in the Easter vigil all the more effective.

The Second Reading

I am considering the second reading last because it does not fit with any of the others. Not that it is a modern intrusion into the Mass; the reading of an "Epistle" as well as a "Gospel" is an ancient feature. Traditionally the two readings were done from different places, the Epistle on the south side (to the right, as the congregation sees it) and the Gospel on the north (to the left), hence the sides of the sanctuary were regularly named "Epistle side" and "Gospel side". The letters of St. Paul and the other apostles have always been valued as the earliest commentaries on the Gospel story, though many will agree with St. Peter that Paul can be a little hard to follow (2 Pet 3:16).

Except on a very few days of the year, the Epistle readings were not chosen with any reference to the other readings. As a result, if you or the preacher can find any connection, this is pure chance, or rather, since very few things happen by chance, pure grace. Fundamentally the idea is to read through each of the Epistles consecutively, so that this Sunday's reading will follow on last Sunday's, in the same way that the Gospels are read. Unlike the Gospels, however, the Epistles do not come apart easily into "pericopes", and a single thought may have to be spread over two or three Sundays. It would be remarkable if anyone who came to the Sunday extract quite unprepared could really understand and appreciate the point of the reading. To make anything of our preparation for Sunday Mass, we will need to look at the Epistle extract in context and get all the help we can from the commentaries.

To read and prepare all this makes quite a lot of hard work before Sunday Mass. It has not generally been noticed that with the introduction of the "new Mass" the Church actually makes much greater demands on us than before. It was possible in the old days to come straight into church unprepared and to fall quickly into contemplative prayer; now we need to do our homework if we are going to get value out of the vocal prayer of the new Mass. Obviously the more accustomed we are to it, the less time needs to be spent in immediate preparation. If we have a knowledge of the whole Bible and have been coming to Mass regularly for years, we will respond to the readings much more easily. But if you are new to the Mass, or still finding it difficult to follow, then a time of preparation (perhaps as a family) can be most effective.

The Feast-Day Readings

Another sequence of readings has been provided for weekday festivals. The most important, and those that draw the greatest crowds, like Christmas or the Sacred

Heart, are treated exactly like Sundays with three readings, a psalm and an Alleluia. On these days, called *Solemnities*, all the texts are selected with reference to the occasion, and for several of the greatest days there is a three-year cycle. Less important but still significant *Feasts* have only one reading before the Gospel, which may be either an Epistle or an Old Testament passage. On these and similar occasions, either the psalm or the Alleluia verse may be used; it is not necessary to use both, though most parishes do. On Feasts at least one of the readings may be directly relevant to the saint or mystery concerned, especially if it is the day of an apostle or another biblical figure.

Most saints are commemorated by *Memorials,* when technically the weekday reading should be used, not anything special for the saint. However a saint who may only have a memorial in the general calendar might be especially popular in a particular country, diocese, or parish and be upgraded to a Feast or even Solemnity. For instance St. Augustine of Canterbury, only a Memorial elsewhere, is a Feast in England, Our Lady of Guadalupe is a feast in the U.S., and a solemnity in Mexico, and St. Frideswide, totally unknown to most of the world, gets a great reception in Oxford. In these cases special readings may be provided for use in that area. For every category of saint, a selection of readings and psalms is found in the Lectionary, from which a sequence suitable for the occasion are chosen.

The Lectionary provides readings for many saints in the calendar, and the "common" readings are available when the parish is celebrating a "local" saint. What this means is that for most days of the year, the priest and readers have the option either of using the weekday cycle (of which more presently) or of using the suggested readings for the saint of the day. My own practice is to look at both sets and see which seems most appropriate. But this freedom of choice means that it is not easy for the congregation to know in advance what readings are coming up and makes it all the more important to have good readers at weekday Mass.

The Weekday Cycle

On ferial days, weekdays that are not saints' days, the weekday cycle applies. In the same sort of way as the Sunday cycle, the Gospels are read through in order in a *one*-year cycle, accompanied by a *two*-year cycle of first readings from either Old or New Testament. These first readings go through various books in sequence and are not tied in to the Gospel readings at all. The responsorial psalms are supposed to reflect the first reading; the Alleluia verse looks forward to the Gospel. During the seasons of Advent, Christmastide, Lent, and Easter, there is a one-year cycle for both readings, and the themes of the seasons are kept in mind throughout, usually disrupting the order within the books themselves. These readings are available in a published weekday missal, so you can prepare them beforehand if the priest uses them in preference to the saints' day readings.

Votive and Occasional Masses

On an ordinary day when there is nothing very important happening, the priest can choose to celebrate a *Votive Mass*, in honor of some mystery or saint, for instance, the Sacred Heart or our Lady. Or he may choose an *Occasional Mass*, such as those for peace, for rain, or in time of earthquake. All of these have their own selection of readings and psalms. On many weekdays, the Mass, therefore, may be something of a surprise, but a good priest will keep you informed and introduce the readings when necessary. And if you attend weekday Mass regularly you may be getting to know the Bible well enough to be able to cope with almost any reading.

The Sermon

Having seen how much preparation is necessary for lay people to be able to make sense of the Liturgy of the Word, you can imagine the task that faces the preacher. He is expected to explain the Scriptures to the people, all three readings plus the psalm, and to do so in not more than ten minutes. The task is of course quite impossible, which may explain why many preachers give up altogether. At least now you can be sympathetic!

In reality no one expects the *sermon* at any one Mass to provide a full explanation of even one of the readings, let alone all three. What the *Instruction* does recommend is that the sermon "develop some point of the readings or of another text from the Ordinary or from the Proper of the Mass of the day, and should take into account the mystery being celebrated and the needs proper to the listeners."[3] (It may be worth saying something here about the difference between a "homily" and a "sermon". Really, *homilia* is the Greek for sermon, and *sermo* is the Latin for homily. The idea that there is a subtle difference in content is moonshine; it is simply that since the changes in the Church it has become fashionable to get rid of Latin words and substitute Greek ones.)

[3] GIRM 41.

How to Preach a Sermon

It normally takes six or seven years to train a priest, and the bulk of that time is occupied in giving him the intellectual formation to be able to preach a sermon. He should have become familiar with the whole Bible, know how every point of Catholic teaching on faith and morals relates to the scriptural record and the tradition of the Church, and have the logical training to make valid connections and deductions. As well as that, he should have satisfied his bishop that he is in accord with the teachings of the Church and has been called to receive the *charism,* or grace, of the Holy Spirit imparted in ordination to enable him to carry out this vital priestly function. All of which goes to show that the idea of lay people preaching is about as silly as unskilled people being asked to do brain surgery; if it takes seven years to train someone to do a job, and even then not all of us are that brilliant at it, how could you do it without any training whatever? The 1997 Instruction on the role of the laity emphasizes this point and stresses that the task of preaching is essentially linked to Holy Orders.[4]

It is true that any congregation will contain bright

[4] Congregation for the Clergy, Pontifical Council for the Laity, et al., *Instruction on Certain Questions Regarding the Collaboration of the Non-Ordained Faithful in the Sacred Ministry of Priests* (Vatican City, August 15, 1997).

lay people who may be experts in one area of knowledge or another. I often have to preach in front of
some of the most profound philosophers in England.
But a sermon is not a lecture, and the Mass is not a
university seminar. The sermon at Mass has to be
accessible to everyone, the grocer as much as the
philosopher, the wandering tramp as much as the
professor. The priest draws on his academic training,
but it should not show too much! Moreover he has to
be able to speak clearly, project his voice maybe for
three or four Masses on a Sunday, be light enough to
hold people's attention and profound enough to stir
their souls. He should resist the temptation to play on
their emotions or to court popularity with frivolity.

In choosing which point to bring out of the texts of
the Mass, he has to "take into account the mystery
being celebrated and the needs proper to the listeners".[5] That actually gives him plenty of scope; once
he has got to know his congregation, he will know
what they need to hear and can plan a course of
sermons accordingly. Nor is it difficult to link up
almost any topic with the readings of the Sunday or
the season. I have successfully been able to preach
"courses" of sermons covering for instance the seven
sacraments or the Ten Commandments while preserv-
ing a plausible link with the readings of the successive

[5] GIRM 41.

Sundays. But an unpredictable hazard can be the sudden arrival of a *pastoral letter* from the bishop that has to be read out whether it is relevant to the readings or not. Another hazard that has multiplied exceedingly in recent years is that various national commissions and pressure groups declare that a certain Sunday is to be devoted to their particular cause and try to knock out the liturgical season or the readings altogether.

Some priests find it easy to preach from brief notes or none, while others prefer to have a written text. Famous preachers have been found in both traditions: Cardinal Newman as a Catholic usually spoke from brief jottings; Msgr. Ronald Knox always wrote his sermons out in full. When a certain bishop criticized Knox for having to use a written text, he sighed in agreement, "I am bitterly conscious of my disability, my Lord. Only the other day a friend remarked, 'When I saw you go into the pulpit with a sheaf of papers I thought we were in for another of those dreadful Pastorals.'"[6]

How to Listen to a Sermon

I have outlined the task that faces the preacher so that you can have some idea of what goes into that sermon

[6] Evelyn Waugh, *The Life of the Right Reverend Ronald Knox* (London: Chapman & Hall, 1959), p. 121 n.

that you find so difficult to appreciate. A good way of preparing for Mass might indeed be to try to work out what sort of sermon you would preach and then compare it with what you get.

Keeping your mind on a sermon can be very difficult indeed, even if you have prepared yourself. Churches are noisy places; there may be children or coughers, interference on the loudspeaker from passing taxis, or an airplane flying overhead. If the preacher is not standing high enough for you to be able to see his lips, it can be much more difficult to hear if you are slightly deaf. Inevitably you will miss something, but do not worry; the priest has probably repeated the main point three times for that very reason. And remember always that the surface of the mind is not the most important part of your attention; a great deal can sink into the subconscious and be of real benefit to your spiritual life without apparently going through your conscious mind at all! The story is told of a novice monk in Egypt long ago who complained to his abbot that he could never retain anything at all of the sermons he heard or the books he read. The abbot said nothing but gave him a dirty basket covered with mud and told him to fill it at the Nile and bring the water back. The novice, knowing that Egyptian abbots were in the habit of asking impossibilities and as often as not working miracles to make up, trotted off to the Nile, filled the basket, and came back. No water remained, so the abbot told him to try again. Again the water ran out, and he was sent back a third time. Finally the abbot asked him: "What have you retained?" "Nothing", said the novice. "Indeed," said the abbot, "but the basket is now clean."

The Creed

The sermon leads rather surprisingly into the *Creed*, or Profession of Faith. It often seems like an intrusion into the Mass, and so indeed it is; it was added at the behest of one of the emperors a thousand years ago, out of a laudable desire to unite the people in proclaiming their loyalty to the faith. Only gradually did it become a standard part of the Mass. Now the *Instruction* tells us that the Creed serves as "a way for the people to respond and to give their assent to the word of God heard in the readings and through the homily."[7]

The text normally used at Mass is the *Nicene-Constantinopolitan Creed*. This has its origin in the great controversies of the fourth century. A significant portion of Christendom had come to deny that Jesus was really God. The more subtle ones thought he was a created being superior to the angels but definitely not

[7] GIRM 43.

God, although rather like him; the simpler folk just thought he was a good man. Loosely speaking, this formed the Arian heresy, and the bishops of the universal Church met at Nicaea in A.D. 325 to agree on what Catholics really did believe. They summed up their conclusions in the Profession of Faith we call the Nicene Creed, which was then circulated as a test or standard of correct belief. The heretics refused to submit, so the bishops met again at Constantinople in 381 and slightly expanded the Creed into the version we use now—all except two words, which had to be added at the Council of Florence a thousand years later!

Because it was the proclamation of faith of a large number of bishops in general councils, the original text began *pistevomen*, "we believe". When it was put into Latin and incorporated into the Mass it was made more personal, *Credo*, "I believe" (hence the English word "creed"), by analogy with the baptismal creed that each Christian recites as a personal undertaking.

The Creed is not only a statement, it is also a prayer. We are offering ourselves to the faith, praying to be strengthened and encouraged in each part of it, praying to be made one with the "Church which still that Faith doth keep". It is not necessary to understand the complicated theological points developed in the Councils of Nicaea and Constantinople in order to assent to the fundamental teaching of the Creed that

Jesus really is God. Every time we switch on the electric light we make an act of assent to theories in physics that most of us cannot understand; we don't know how the light works but we trust that it will. In the same way in the Creed we assent to the faith that works even if the actual workings are a bit complicated.

Because the Creed dates from fourth-century controversies, it says little or nothing about the important developments in Christian doctrine that have come since, but no one has seriously suggested lengthening the Mass by making us recite the whole *Credo of the People of God* or the Catechism. Basically once we have professed our faith in one, holy, catholic and apostolic Church, everything that the Church teaches is contained in that assent. By joining in the Creed, we are accepting the teaching and unity of the Catholic Church in their entirety.

Normally the Creed is recited in unison by the whole congregation. It is, however, one of the few parts of the Mass that is still commonly sung in Latin, using the rather late plainsong setting known as "Credo III". It is extraordinary how that setting can be started at an international gathering of Catholics from all over the world and then be taken up in a full-bodied roar that really displays the unity of the Church. There are of course many other Latin settings of the Creed (Credo I is supposed to be the normal one), including the Bach B minor setting that was written for the beginning of a school term and takes half an hour. Singing the Creed in English has not really caught on yet, though some settings are available. I have a record of a Zimbabwean choir singing it in chiShona as a responsory; the leader states the various propositions of the Creed, and the choir respond with a resonant "Yes, I believe." Perhaps something like that could be attempted in European languages; the Creed should be something rather triumphant and assertive, and it is rather difficult to do that with a long text spoken in unison.

In Masses with children, the *Apostles' Creed* may be used instead. This is an older text and has its origin in the rite of baptism. It is the Profession of Faith to be made by or on behalf of the new Christian and, as a personal statement, always begins "I believe". Clearly the Nicene-Constantinopolitan Creed was derived from the tradition of the Apostles' Creed, and it seems to be a matter of the bishop's preference which is used.

The Prayer of the Faithful

On a weekday (unless it is a solemnity) the Creed is omitted, and the sermon leads directly into prayer, the prayers of intercession in which we ask God for the needs of the Church and the world. On a Sunday it seems more disjointed as we turn back from a confident profession of faith to the more tentative prayers of intercession. Indeed, there was a time when the Prayer of the Faithful came before the Creed; many parts of the Mass have moved around over the centuries, and there is no reason to think they have definitively come to rest yet.

The intercessions are called the *Prayer of the Faithful* because at one stage in the evolution of the Mass they marked the beginning of the "Mass of the Faithful", the secret ceremony that only baptized Catholics in good standing could attend; strangers, catechumens, and penitents were expected to leave at this point, and in some rites of Mass they are still encouraged to do so. In Eastern churches there are several sets of intercessions, introduced by the deacon, "again and again in peace let us pray to the Lord", in which first the whole congregation and then only the faithful join in prayer for different intentions, responding "Lord have mercy" to each petition. In the Western Church, this tradition generally fell out of use and in the Roman rite survived just as a token greeting between priest and people and the invitation "let us pray". In some dioceses of France the prayers survived as the *prône* for the living and the dead, before the Creed. In the mediæval English rite, the prayers, called the *bidding prayers*, came much later after the Offertory.

As introduced in the 1960s, the Prayer of the Faithful consists of an invitation by the priest, several intercessions read by the deacon or substitute, and a concluding collect again by the priest. The texts are not printed in the Missal in the natural place (as they are in the Eastern and older rites), but eleven sets of prayers are given at the back. These are called "samples": the implication is that prayers should be newly composed for each occasion on the models given. This is done in some parishes, with greater or lesser success. Other parishes subscribe to books or leaflets giving pre-prepared prayers composed for every Sunday of the three-year cycle. In some countries sets are available for every weekday Mass as well. Some priests use the intercessory prayers from morning or evening prayer found in the breviary.

The *Instruction* provides a sequence for the intercessions: "a) for the needs of the Church; b) for public authorities and the salvation of the world; c) for those oppressed by any need; d) for the local community."[8] The prayer for the Pope and local bishop should be included under (a), that for the President or other head of state under (b), as should international crises and wars. The sick, if possible naming members of the congregation, come under (c), and local concerns, children preparing for the sacraments, and so on, under

---

[8] GIRM 46

(d), which also includes prayers for the dead, recent deaths in the parish, and anniversaries. The problem with the pre-prepared books of prayers is that they cannot easily be changed to take account of local needs, sudden disasters, and matters of great concern to the particular congregation. The opposite extreme has been tried in some places of making the prayers up on the spot or even inviting the congregation to chip in. This can lead to the "news bulletin" sort of prayer, when everyone competes to be the first to make up a prayer in response to some piece of news they have just heard on the radio. It can also lead to the wry comment, "The Lord may graciously hear you, but I can't." It is important in public worship that anything intended for the whole congregation to hear and respond to should be audible and accessible to everyone, which does seem to demand that the intercessions should be clearly proclaimed and prepared in advance so that they do hold together and avoid absurdities and risky political tendencies.

An English speciality, which is beginning to catch on in other countries, is to include an invocation to our Lady and the common recital of the Hail Mary. This seems to have been the initiative of a single archbishop, concerned at the tendency to ignore or exclude our Lady from public worship; it reminds us that just as salvation came into the world through her, so all our prayers and needs are still her concern, and that as Mother of the Church, she leads us in our prayers. The tradition is now deeply rooted and has contributed to the restoration of our Lady's natural place close to the heart of our worship.

The *Instruction* expects the Prayer of the Faithful to be inserted into every public Mass. In practice it is usually omitted on weekdays, though it can be shortened to a very brief invitation to pray for all the needs of the world and, in particular, for the intention for which the Mass is being offered. The congregation "gives expression to its supplication either by a response said together after each intention or by silent prayer", so the Hail Mary can be used as the common response after such a brief invitation to prayer.

Since the Prayer of the Faithful forms the conclusion of the Liturgy of the Word, it is understood to be the response to readings and sermon, and ideally in its wording it will take up themes and phrases from the readings as well as points from the homily. That seems to mean that the preacher should normally compose the prayers. (I remember one embarrassing incident in my student days when the invited guest preacher had strongly emphasized a point that was flatly contradicted by the first invocation in the Prayers of the Faithful prepared by a student.) If the prayers are not well chosen and introduced, the ordinary member of the congregation may have to make a general intention of praying with the Church without worrying too much about the specific points being made. Properly composed prayers, on the other hand, can very much help people to focus their intentions. It does make a difference if the guidelines in the *General Instruction* are followed.

5

Coming before Jesus: The Offertory

The Second Table

We have fed at the Table of the Word; now the time
has come to prepare the Table of the Sacrament. There
is a change of focus, a change of direction. The "two
tables" are "so closely connected that they form but
one single act of worship";[1] they form together parts of
a single whole, but we should be able to see a clear
progression from one to another. The position and
posture of priest and people should make this clear.
During the Liturgy of the Word, the readers and
preacher are addressing the people. Information is
being transmitted from an authoritative source (the
Word) to the listeners (the People). It is obviously
appropriate for the readers and preacher to face the
people they are addressing and for the people to be in

[1] GIRM 8; cf SC 56.

a posture of attentive listening. Hence the readings and sermon are delivered from a lectern, ambo, or pulpit facing the congregation and high enough for all to see the speaker. The people for the most part sit to listen, except only that they stand to greet the words of Jesus Himself in the Gospel. During the Liturgy of the Word, the congregation is essentially passive; even when the people join in singing the psalm, this is in a passive, receptive mood; only the readers, preacher, and lead singers are active. It is natural that the arrangement of the church during this part of the Mass should be not unlike a classroom or lecture theater.

All this changes when we come to the sacrifice. Now priest and people together are joining in an action of worship. Worship means prayer, acknowledging the presence and the authority of God, surrendering ourselves and all we have back into his hands and receiving from him far more than we can possibly hope to give. The priest is no longer the learned authority; he is the go-between, the ambassador between God and his people. The very word *priest* is linked to the Greek for "ambassador" (2 Cor 5:20). The personality of the priest should no longer be noticeable; like a diplomat, he is to have no words or ideas of his own but is to speak only on behalf of those he represents. When he offers presents on behalf of the people, he is standing forth as their spokesman; when he brings the Presence of God back to the people, he speaks in the very Name of God.

Because of this, the tradition of the Church had always been that the priest leads his people, standing before them and facing, with them, toward the Rising Sun, to present the sacrifice on their behalf. Very often in the past this was emphasized, as it was in the Old Testament Temple, by a ceremonial entry to the Holy Place. The priest, bearing the gifts, would leave the crowd of worshippers and pass through a door or a veil toward the East. And then he would return as God's ambassador, coming back through the doors or the veils to bring the Gifts to the people. The people join in the prayer, all kneeling, facing east, pouring out their hearts in love towards God and eager to receive God's Gifts. The people are active in this prayer even though for the most part silent. A recent innovation has been the practice of celebrating the Mass "facing the people". This was based partly on a mistaken idea of what happened in the early Church: there are some ancient churches where the altar stands in such a position that the priest must have stood behind it looking toward the body of the church. It was imagined that the people would have stood in the body of the church facing toward the priest. In fact we now know that in these churches the people stood in the transepts, or *bema,* on either side of the priest, and all faced east together; the altars faced down the church solely because that was the direction of the sunrise.

The result of this mistake is that the "classroom" arrangement of the church persists throughout the whole Mass, and the priest always appears to be the dominant personality speaking at the people. This frustrates the intention of the Second Vatican Council to organize the Mass "so that the specific nature of each part should be be more clearly seen as well as their relationship to each other".[2] It is generally agreed to have been inappropriate that in the past the readings were read by the priest facing away from the people, so that they did not get the impression they were being instructed; now it seems equally inappropriate that the *Eucharistic Prayer*, in which the priest makes the offering on behalf of the people, should be directed to their faces. The difference between the two tables of the Mass is more clearly seen if the priest and readers face toward the people while instructing them and face the same way as the people when leading them in worship toward God. Much of our young people's disillusionment about the Mass is because it appears to be a continuous monologue of the dominant priest, projecting himself toward the people.

Having said that, in virtually all churches we are faced with a "forward altar", and the whole Mass will be celebrated facing west, at least for the foreseeable future. We just need to remember that from the

---

[2] SC 50.

offertory onward the priest is no longer speaking to the congregation; he is speaking to God on behalf of the congregation.

What Is a Priest?

At this point it may be appropriate to reflect on what it is that essentially makes a *priest*. It has become customary to refer to him as the "president", which carries with it unfortunate connotations in English. We think of a president as the chief magistrate of a republic, somebody dependant on popular election and endowed with considerable power and prestige as long as he remains acceptable to the electorate. While he is president, he dominates and controls everything. Once out of office, he becomes a private citizen again.

None of this applies to a Catholic priest, which may be why none of the official documents of the Church, neither those of Vatican II nor the *General Instruction*, ever uses the word "president". The word seems to derive from an inaccurate translation of St. Justin's *Apologia*, where "president" is used to represent the Greek word *proestos,* which means "the one who stands in front". The priest stands in front of the people; he also stands in front of God; what he does not do is sit on a great throne and dominate the proceedings. He is not elected by the people but by God; his authority does not come "from below" but "from above". It is clear from the Gospels that Jesus chose some, but not all, of his disciples to be apostles, and he gave them their authority, breathing on them and giving them the Holy Spirit. It is clear from the Acts of the Apostles that these same apostles passed on this commission and Holy Spirit to chosen men. This is how priests have been ordained ever since. They are not chosen by people for their intelligence, eloquence, or good looks but are called by God to perform a specific function that comes on them from the Holy Spirit and is not taken away from them as if the Holy Spirit had made a mistake.

This has the double effect of enhancing the position of the priest and diminishing his personality. Like St. John the Baptist, he prays, "He must increase, but I must decrease." The priest is not there to dominate the Church but to serve her and, in so doing, to become more like Jesus Christ, who came not to be served but to serve. Other people may be far better qualified to teach (most Catholic teachers in the past have been women) or to read in public (which is why the office of reader exists), to organize ceremonies (most priests are hopeless as "MCs") or to run the finances and administration of the parish (lay trustees, treasurers, and administrators have always been more effective). What the priest, and only the priest, can do is to stand before God on behalf of the people and offer gift and sacrifice.

An ambassador is appointed by the sovereign to speak for the nation with authority; a private individual who pretended to be an ambassador would be laughed out of the chanceries of Europe. And the ambassador can bring back an answer to the sovereign with the right to be present and to be heard in a way that others cannot. The analogy is only partial and must not be stretched too far, but if you think of the priest as diplomat rather than politician you will be nearer the mark.

The Liturgy of the Word is something that can be delegated. Almost anyone can read the Bible to others; almost anyone can be trained to teach. There are, and always have been, occasions when in the absence of a priest suitable lay people can conduct services of the Word to instruct the people and help them to pray. In mission territories this has been the traditional role of the catechist. The recent Vatican Instruction on the laity stresses that "a special mandate of the bishop is necessary for the non-ordained members of the faithful to lead such such celebrations",[3] and it makes a clear distinction between services of the Word in the absence of the priest and the Holy Mass, at which an ordained bishop, priest or deacon alone can preach.[4] The Liturgy of the Word can exist on its own without

[3] Congregation for the Clergy, Pontifical Council for the Laity, et al., *Instructions on certain Questions Regarding the Collaboration of the Non-ordained Faithful in the Sacred Ministry of Priests* (Vatican City, August, 1997), art. 7.

[4] Ibid, art. 2.

the rest of the Mass and can be entirely conducted by lay people; it will not be found very exciting, especially for the young, but it can be done. The Liturgy of the Eucharist, on the other hand, should never be done on its own, and cannot be done at all without a priest. The Word prepares and instructs the faithful, making their hearts burn within them, so that they are able to recognize Jesus in the breaking of bread.

A Silent Interval

After the torrent of words there comes a moment of stillness and silence as the altar is prepared for the Sacrifice of the Mass. It often seems rather like a theater intermission; everyone sits down and relaxes, and ushers go up and down the aisles taking money. You almost expect a safety curtain to be lowered. In fact, various important things are going on, and this part, the *Offertory*, has always been considered one of the essential actions of the Mass. Paradoxically, although it looks like the passive, quiet moment, it is really the moment of most activity, as priest and people offer themselves, dedicating their whole lives again to God, abandoning themselves to divine providence.

The Offertory Procession

A symbolic action takes place to represent this self-oblation of the people. A procession is formed, often accompanied by candles, in which bread, wine, and water are carried through the congregation toward the altar. In some parishes the collection of money is also carried in this procession. This is theoretically ideal, but it does mean that there has to be quite a long pause while the collection is taken up before the procession can start. Because of this, in other parishes the collectors come up in the procession with empty baskets and begin to take up the collection after the other gifts have been handed over, returning later in a second procession to present their takings. A method I have seen in the United States and Africa is for the whole congregation to take part in the procession: all come forward and throw their money offering into a basket at the altar steps. If they are intending to receive Communion, they also transfer an altar bread from a container into the ciborium. This sort of procession, in which all come forward to present their gifts before the altar, seems to have biblical precedent and was certainly used in mediæval England. You may remember Chaucer's Wife of Bath got frightfully upset if anyone got into the procession in front of her:

In al the parisshe wif ne was ther noon
That to the offrynge bifore hire sholde goon;

And if ther dide, certeyn so wrooth was she,
That she was out of alle charitee.
(*Canterbury Tales*, General Prologue, 449–52)

The purpose of the procession is rather obscured by the fact that everyone knows the bread and wine have only just been placed at the back of the church before Mass and that they have been provided by the priest. Usually the altar boys have the task of carrying the gifts to the back of the church, and their sisters bring them back again. They may be accompanied by children bringing their drawings for Father to look at or items being brought up for distribution to the poor. What does it all mean? Fundamentally the idea is that the materials for the sacrifice of the Mass should be seen to have been given by the people. The Mass is not something performed in front of them; it is *their* sacrifice. Actually the money is the most important part of the procession: the bread and wine have been purchased out of "parish funds", as has the church building itself, and these funds come from nowhere but the people. It is the offertory collection that pays for altar and sanctuary, for benches and candles, that keeps the congregation out of the rain and feeds the priest for them. By giving to the collection, the people make themselves part of the parish; they gain a sort of "ownership" of the church and all its works; they surrender part of themselves to receive much more in return.

The procession should, therefore, include the money collection (and the oldest account of the Mass we possess does mention this feature) and should also include the "consumables" to be used at the Mass, that is, the bread, wine, water, and also the candles. It does not make much sense to send up a chalice, which has been purchased long ago and has been in use already, but it does make sense to bring new church vessels up in the procession to be blessed and used for the first time. Bringing up children's drawings is not really appropriate and contributes to the schoolroom atmosphere that so many young people find stifling; but it does make sense for the children to bring up toys for refugee children or groceries to be distributed to the poor. For the offertory collection in past ages was not always taken in coin but could include fruit and vegetables, all sorts of produce and artifacts not only to support the clergy but also for them to distribute to those in need. It was one of the early functions of the deacon to cope with this mountain of groceries, to place them beside the altar to be blessed during Mass, and to distribute them afterward. (I remember seeing my brother one Sunday when he had no money putting a box of eggs in the collection instead—I do not think the priest appreciated it, but it was liturgically correct!)

The Offertory Chant

During the marshaling of the procession, and as it advances up the church, there may be a chant, hymn, or motet. It was intended that there should be another responsorial psalm at this point. When that was dropped, an antiphon should have been provided as for the Introit. Through an oversight, the antiphons were not provided, so there are no official texts for the offertory chant. Most churches choose a hymn, with the theme of offering, giving, and self-surrender. In large churches this may be followed by a choir motet or organ music until the end of the whole Offertory. The effect should be relaxing and peaceful, giving the congregation a rest after the Liturgy of the Word and preparing them for the sacrifice.

Preparing the Altar

Meanwhile the servers, and deacon if available, should have made the altar ready to receive the gifts. In theory during the opening rites and Liturgy of the Word, the altar should stand empty, decently covered with white cloths and perhaps a colored frontal appropriate to the season, but without books or vessels. The Missal on its stand or cushion should now be placed so that it is to the priest's left, and the chalice and paten with the corporal brought from the side table. The corporal, the square of white linen, is laid flat on the altar and carefully unfolded; if it has been properly put away, it will unfold so that the edge with the little red cross is nearest the priest. The paten is placed on the corporal, the chalice somewhere to its right, and the purificator and pall on the altar beside it. If necessary the microphone is placed near the Missal. (Are microphones really necessary? Every word the priest speaks at the altar is to be found in the Missal, so deaf parishioners can easily follow what he says. Using a microphone throughout the Mass does rather contribute to the "barrage of words" effect that can often be more of a distraction than a help.)

The Bread

When the offertory procession arrives, priest and servers greet it at the altar step and take the gifts. The collection baskets are placed at the foot of the altar or on a side table; the bread, wine, and water are brought to the altar itself. The ciborium containing the altar breads is placed on the corporal, and the priest extracts the one large host and lays it on the paten. Then holding the paten and ciborium slightly above the altar, the priest recites the little prayer of blessing. At a Mass without music, it is permissible for the priest to say this little blessing prayer and the similar one over the chalice aloud; in fact, the English version of the Missal provides a response for the people. This was not actually intended when the new Mass was devised, and many parishes are now finding that it is more effective to keep the offertory silent up to the words "pray, brethren". The offertory prayers have taken many forms over the centuries and have varied more than any other part of the Roman rite. The present ones, added at the last minute during the 1969 revision, derive from the Jewish family grace before meals, thanking God for his goodness in providing us with food and drink.

The Wine

The priest turns to his right to prepare the chalice, unless there is a deacon who will have done this already. Wine is poured in and mixed with a little water, accompanied by a prayer that draws attention to the mingling of human and divine nature in Christ, asking that we should share his divinity in the same way that he shares our humanity. This prayer, a cut-down version of the one in the old Missal, derives from the teaching of the early Fathers, particularly St. Athanasius, who summed up the whole of our faith in the proclamation "The Son of God became man so that we might become God."[5] The mixing of wine and water was actually a feature of ancient life generally; only hopeless drunkards drank wine neat, and the chances are that at the Last Supper the wine would have been heavily diluted, as it was even at Plato's notorious drinking party. Although theologians agree that a proportion of up to one to two is permissible, nowadays only a very little water is mixed in, and in some parishes a small spoon is used to ensure that only a few drops of water are added. (The spoon is actually one of the oldest of church vessels but was originally perforated to strain out the skins and pips from the wine; there is a fine fourth-century example on display in the British Museum.) In parishes where Communion is also distributed to the congregation from the chalice, it will be necessary to have two or more chalices, all prepared in the same way.

The wine is offered by the priest with another little prayer of blessing, and he then bows to invoke God's acceptance of the offering. At a solemn Mass the gifts are then incensed. The thurible and incense boat are brought forward, the priest places incense on the charcoal and blesses it, and he takes the thurible to make the gesture of incensation first over the bread and wine, then to the cross, and then around the altar. He is then incensed in his turn, and the deacon or server

[5] *De Incarnatione* 54, 3 (PG 25, 192B).

proceed to give the same honor to the people. Those being incensed rise and bow to the thurifer before and after the incensation. We are reminded that those in the congregation are themselves the Mystical Body of Christ, the Church, and worthy of veneration on that account.

The Lavabo

The priest then washes his hands, with the assistance of the servers. This is no empty gesture: after handling the cruets of wine, his hands are likely to be sticky, especially if he has also been using the thurible. In hot weather generous hand washing becomes essential. After this washing the priest as far as possible touches nothing save the host and chalice; he may well keep his thumbs and forefingers together except when touching the host to ensure that they remain scrupulously clean. Again this is no empty gesture: he is going to handle the Hosts that the people will receive with these fingers, and courtesy to the people as well as to our Lord demands that his fingers be clean. Yet there is also a symbolic meaning to the hand washing expressed in another cut-down prayer, replacing the scriptural text "Lavabo inter innocentes manus meas" (I will wash my hands among the innocent) from which the word *lavabo* derives. It is a prayer that the priest, while conscious of his own sinfulness, may be washed clean and purified from stain of sin.

Invitation to Prayer

Returning to the center of the altar, the priest waits until the end of any music that may be in progress and then breaks the stillness with the invitation "pray, brethren". It invites the people to claim ownership of the sacrifice: it is *their* sacrifice. But they are also invited to acknowledge that the priest is acting on their behalf in offering it to God: it is *his* sacrifice. Both congregation and priest actually offer the sacrifice, but in different ways: they give the materials; they give themselves; they come before God in worship; he accepts the gifts from them and passes them on to God; he is the go-between; he is the representative who stands before God on behalf of the people. The response to the priest's invitation to prayer gives the whole congregation's assent to what is being done for them and expresses their faith that the sacrifice will be of benefit not only for themselves but for the whole of God's People, living and dead. There is a great deal of theology packed into that short exchange of dialogue.

What Is a Sacrifice?

In modern English we use the word *sacrifice* to mean "giving something up" or depriving ourselves of something of our own for a good reason. That is not at all what the word means in the Bible. In our English Bibles the common word "sacrifice" represents half a dozen different ceremonies described in the Old Law, in the books of Exodus, Leviticus, Numbers, and Deuteronomy. What they all have in common is that it is God who is giving something to his people, not the other way around. The word "sacrifice" means "making holy". The gifts used in the sacrifice are made holy in order that those who consume them become holy themselves. The typical sacrifice for the Christian Mass was the *Passover:* the Jewish family would choose a lamb, a good specimen, one of the best of that year's lambing. They would "offer" it to God, that is, come before God with prayer, asking him to bless the lamb, to make it holy, to make it a token of his forgiveness and favor. The lamb would be killed, and the blood (which symbolized its life) would be poured out before God to represent the pouring out of the lives of the people in service to their loving God. And then all would cook and eat the lamb. By sharing in this lamb of sacrifice, the lamb that had been made holy, all the people were made holy; they were conscious that they had been chosen, forgiven, and loved by God and that through eating the holy lamb, their sins had been taken away. So a sacrifice is not the people's gift to God (how could we give him anything?) but God's gift to the people. The lamb was the vehicle of God's grace, chosen to represent all the good things God had given his people. By offering the lamb they called down God's favor, focused on this one lamb but, through it, made the whole flock holy. By eating the lamb, they took God's grace into themselves and became the holy People of God. When the Church uses the word "sacrifice" in the Mass, we mean very much the same thing, except that, as we shall see, the lamb is replaced by Jesus Christ himself.

The Prayer over the Gifts

In response to the people's prayer of sacrifice, the priest prays the second of the three prayers of the Mass, another "collect", which sums up the hopes and aspirations of all the people. Like the Opening Prayer, this one is chosen from the Missal for the day, the season, or the particular occasion. The text is likely to emphasize the action of offering, the joining of priest and people in the presentation of the gifts before God. Because this prayer is said over the "things set aside", which in Latin are *secreta*, it used to be called the "secret" prayer. Apparently, however, it was never really meant to be said secretly, although for many centuries this was the case. As with all these collects, the people express their assent with the acclamation "Amen!" which brings to an end the Offertory rite.

6

Jesus Is Made Present: The Consecration

Rising in expectant attention, the congregation stands as the priest begins the *Preface*, the introduction to the Eucharistic Prayer. After its acclamation, the *Sanctus*, all fall to their knees in adoration for the central, most important part of the Mass, the *Canon*. This is what really constitutes the Mass; this is the focus and source of the Catholic faith.

The Preface

The priest and congregation exchange a brief passage of dialogue that is the oldest set text found in the Mass. First come mutual greetings and good wishes in the Lord, "The Lord be with you", as we have heard already several times. Then we are invited to turn to the Lord in prayer, "Lift up your hearts". It seems that it was at this moment in the early Church that all turned and faced east if they were not already doing so.

Our faith came from the east; it was heralded by a star rising in the east; Christ is called the Rising Sun; we look toward the dawn, sign of new light and hope springing into a darkened world. And Christ will come "like lightning rising in the east and flashing over to the west" (Mt 24:27). "Let us give thanks" is our invitation to join in the Eucharist, for the Greek for thanks was (and still is) *evcharisto*. The supreme act of Christian worship is called thanksgiving, *eucharist,* because it is our response to a gift greater than ourselves. We cannot repay God for what he has done for us; all we can do is thank him. And it is no accident that the central element in the word *eucharist* is *charis,* which means grace, favor, or beauty. God has made us beautiful by his grace, chosen us, favored us: we can only respond with graceful, grateful thanks, "charis in return for charis", as St. John puts it (Jn 1:16).

The *Preface* is, as its name implies, an introductory prayer, which gives a specific reason for our thanksgiving. The Roman Missal now contains no fewer than eighty-one Prefaces, and there are many more in particular supplements to the Missal, for instance, the Preface of St. Philip Neri for the Oratorians or several special ones for Masses of our Lady in the Marian supplement. The choice of Preface is dependent on the day, the season, or the occasion. Some are fixed: that for the Annunciation or the Sacred Heart, for the Easter vigil or Pentecost Sunday.

On other occasions there is a limited choice, for instance, there are four more Prefaces of Eastertide that can be used after the Easter octave as alternatives to the first Easter Preface; there are several for feasts of apostles. On other days there is a wider range: eight possibilities for ordinary Sundays, six for weekdays. If the priest is opting for a votive Mass, there will be a suitable Preface, as there is for a feast of each of the different categories of saints. Finally there are three Prefaces for wedding Masses, and five for funerals, and so forth.

In making the choice of Preface, the priest is guided not only by specific recommendations in the Missal but by his judgment of which Preface fits in best with the readings or the theme of his sermon. A special case is the Preface to Canon IV, which belongs solely to that Canon, which cannot be used without it. There is a Preface that particularly belongs to Canon II, but they are not inseparably linked. Additional Canons for Children or Reconciliation also have particular and inseparable Prefaces, so in effect the choice of Preface only applies if the priest is using one of the first three Canons. (It is unfortunate that many publishers of missalettes take it on themselves to choose Prefaces, usually just rotating them in a mechanical way with no reference to the readings.)

What all Prefaces have in common is that they begin by addressing God the Father, picking up the words of the congregational response to the invitation to pray. We do well to give thanks always and everywhere, and this thanksgiving is made through our Lord Jesus Christ, who is mentioned at this point in most Prefaces.

The middle paragraph of the Preface gives the theme or motive for thanksgiving, referring to the occasion, season, or saint or giving a general summary of some vital part of our faith. The form of the prayer in English gives the impression that we are informing or reminding God of something, but of course it is we who need to be informed or reminded by him. As so often in our prayers, we should not think so much that we are addressing God as that he is addressing us through the medium of our prayer. In nearly every Preface there is a specific mention of Jesus Christ and usually of the Holy Spirit as well.

The closing paragraph then sums up our praise and thanksgiving, leading into a song of acclamation, the "unending hymn of praise". Most Prefaces are explicit in naming the angels as joining in that praise, for at this point we must imagine the veils between earth and heaven to be growing thin.

The original concept of worship, enshrined in the Temple at Jerusalem and in Christian churches ever since, is that we try to model our earthly prayer on the eternal praise of heaven. The veil, screen, or gate represents the barrier between heaven and earth; the

Preface is the moment when the priest symbolically disappears through that barrier to bring the prayers and offerings of the people into the court of heaven. The people singing outside are answered by the choir singing inside, as if heaven is now so close that the voices of angels are audible. In our present Western Mass, none of this is at all clear, but the singing of the *Sanctus* occurs still at this place as a reminder of the high worship of the past.

The Sanctus

The little acclamation we call the *Sanctus* (Latin for "holy") is a triumphant chant for angelic and human voices in counterpoint. The first verse is a quotation from the prophet Isaiah. In his opening vision he describes how he penetrated, as it were, through the veils at the Temple liturgy, seeing the reality it symbolized: God on his throne and the ceaseless worship of the seraphim calling to each other "Holy, Holy, Holy!" (Is 6:1–4). It is followed by a quotation from the Gospel, the song of the children of Jerusalem greeting our Lord as he entered his holy city, "Blessed is he who comes in the name of the Lord" (Mt 21:9). The heavenly voices were acclaiming God the Father; the earthly voices greeted Jesus the Son, and we put them together in this chant to proclaim that this Jesus, the man from Galilee, is at the same time the one, eternal, true God.

The *Sanctus* is one of the texts that most needs to be sung, or if recited it needs a firm and exalted tone. The great musical settings of the past are very elaborate, playing voice against voice to represent the antiphonal singing heard by Isaiah or the effect of crowds of children on either side of the road in Jerusalem. Many modern settings are antiphonal, the choir and the congregation answering each other to give more or less the same effect. Like the prophet Isaiah, the congregation kneels in awe, for we realize we are in the presence of something greater than ourselves.

The Canon of the Mass

The priest begins to recite the long Eucharistic Prayer, and all else is silent. Always in the past this prayer was said in a low voice, and the singing of the Sanctus continued over it, dying down into a moment of breathless silence for the Consecration before rising again in the second part, the *Benedictus*. Or in other forms of the Liturgy the priest's voice was raised as the choir grew quieter, so that the words of Consecration would sound clearly in the interval between the singing of the two parts of the Sanctus. Either made a very dramatic impact on the congregation, and it is clear to all that something very important is happening. This is much more difficult to convey now that the Canon seems to be simply a long monologue directed toward the people by the priest. The structure and direction of this part of the Mass are obscured, and the unfortunate result is that many people find this the most boring and featureless part of the Mass. We can recover our sense of prayer and understanding if we have an idea of what is going on and of the meaning of the different parts of the Canon.

Canons and Eucharistic Prayers

In the search for clarity, the short word *Canon* has largely been superceded by the Greek *Eucharistic Prayer* to mean the central prayer of the Mass. *Canon* meant the fixed part, the unchanging and most authoritative part of the Mass, applicable during the centuries when there were many variants of the Western Mass but all agreed on a single text for the Canon. Now that there are several "canons", it seems to make more sense to call them "Eucharistic Prayers", prayers that encapsulate the act of thanksgiving. On the other hand, "canon" is so much shorter and easier to say that it survives in common speech.

There are four Eucharistic Prayers in the English edition of the Roman Missal, and a further five in an appendix or a special supplement. Editions in other languages include some extra prayers, some of which may appear in a future edition of the English version. Yet all the prayers have the same structure more or less, and all effect the same thing. In theory, the priest is to choose the prayer most appropriate for the feast, season, or occasion, using his judgment sometimes at the last minute to decide whether the congregation is so restless and the children so noisy that a short prayer is needed or whether they are quiet and receptive enough for him to use a long one. In practice the choice is often made by the publishers of missalettes who rotate between the first three prayers, having decided that Prayer IV is not "politically correct". In countries where these missalettes are not in common use, the majority of priests seem to have settled for the exclusive use of Canon II on the grounds that it is the shortest.

Parts of the Eucharistic Prayer

The chief elements of a Eucharistic Prayer, according to the *General Instruction*, are (a) thanksgiving, (b) acclamation, (c) epiclesis, (d) institution narrative and Concecration, (e) anamnesis, (f) offering, (g) intercessions, and (h) final doxology.[1] These are all to be found

[1] GIRM 55.

in every prayer, but not always in the same order or in the same relative proportions. (a) Thanksgiving is encapsulated in the Preface, as we have already seen, and the (b) acclamation is the Sanctus. The other parts are found within the main prayers, where we shall look at them.

The Roman Canon

In point of fact Eucharistic Prayer I is the original basic one, also known as the Roman Canon. It is only slightly adapted from the canon used in all Western churches since the end of the Roman Empire, so that as an integral text, it has greater authority and antiquity than the others. It may be used on any occasion and is particularly recommended on the days or during the seasons when there are special texts for parts of the prayer as well as on feasts of apostles and Roman saints and on Sundays generally.[2] The adaptations in the 1960s consisted mainly of reducing the amount of action, ritual gestures, and signs of the cross, because some priests used to do them so carelessly as to make them rather irreverent.

The Roman Canon begins with an echo of the theme of thanksgiving but moves directly into that of (g) intercession. We pray for the Church, naming her

[2] GIRM 322.

servants the Pope and the local bishop. The unity of the Church depends on the mutual recognition of bishops, and the Pope as Bishop of Rome acts as focus and guarantee of that unity. Naming the two prelates is an important and ancient act of asserting our adherence to that unity as well as our loyalty and affection for the individuals concerned. At times in the past when rival popes or bishops might be competing for adherents, it was a crucial test of fidelity to name the right ones. In the older rite of Mass the emperor or the local king would also be named at this place, since the temporal power also was seen as part of the service of God's Church. This custom gradually dwindled away. It is replaced by the intercession for the state in the Prayers of the Faithful.

The intercessions continue with the commemoration of the living. The Mass is offered for all God's people, but the needs of particular people can be emphasized and brought before God at this point. (They are named in silence to avoid embarrassment or jealousy.) We speak loosely of "offering the Mass" for such and such an *intention*, and it is customary for Catholics to ask the priest to say Mass for the intention they request, either for the living or (as we shall come to in due course) for the dead. The custom goes back to St. Paul, who writes to the Thessalonians that he will make the Thanksgiving on their behalf (1 Th 1:2). But the prayer continues to mention all those present and all who are dear to us, for the Mass is too great to be confined to a single intention.

The next paragraph, the *communicantes*, is another assertion of the unity of the Church, this time with those who have gone before us, the saints. The Church not only consists of those now alive on earth (the "Church Militant") but includes also the dead, both those still being purified by God's love (the "Church Suffering") and those who have achieved the final goal of their existence in heaven (the "Church Triumphant"). The chief of these is naturally our Lady, the model and Mother of the Church. Around her gather the twelve apostles, just as they did in the first days after the Ascension (Acts 1:13–14), for the apostles are the foundation stones of the Church. The next named saints are those who begin the succession from the apostles to our own time, the first few popes, and some of the key figures in the earliest days of the Church in Rome. The choice of names is therefore intended to be a list, not of the most popular or best known saints, but of those who are formative of the Church. (The recent addition of St. Joseph, while undoubtedly popular, is actually out of sequence with the structure of the prayer.) We affirm our unity therefore with the Church of the apostles and ask that our prayers may join with theirs.

If the priest is in a hurry, he may omit most of the named saints as well as the conclusion, which offers the prayer, like all others, "through Christ our Lord". On certain occasions there are different opening paragraphs for the *communicantes*: at Christmas, Epiphany, Easter, Ascension, and Pentecost, in each case celebrating the relevant mystery of our faith.

The Epiclesis

The next important element in the Eucharistic Prayer is (c) the *epiclesis*. This Greek word means the calling down of the Holy Spirit to sanctify the gifts, to make them holy, to make them into the Body and Blood of Jesus Christ. In the Roman Canon this is not emphasized as much as in the Eastern Liturgies, and the Holy Spirit is not named, but the gesture of laying on of hands is a silent invocation of the Spirit. The priest calls on God the Father to accept the offering, not only the bread and wine but also the "whole family" that presents them. In other words, the gifts of bread and wine are the vehicles for the self-offering of priest and congregation. God is called on to bless and approve the offering, to make it holy so that we may become holy. Specifically and unambiguously God is called on to transform the offering of bread and wine into the Body and Blood of Jesus Christ.

Again on certain occasions there are alternative versions of this epiclesis prayer. During the week after

Easter, when the newly baptized are supposed to be present, at ordinations, weddings, religious profession, and confirmation, there are specific mentions of those who have been given the sacrament or sacramental and who join in the act of offering.

The Consecration Narrative

Taking first the bread and then the wine, the priest repeats over them our Lord's words and actions at the Last Supper. This is the *Consecration*, the key moment of the Mass. The text is not an exact quotation from any of the four Gospels; indeed, the liturgical version may go straight back to the oral traditions that preceded the actual writing of the Gospels, but it is clearly telling the same story as that told by St Matthew and St Mark. The actual *words of institution*, printed in larger type in all Missals, are the words spoken by Jesus that brought about the radical change in the very nature of things, by which the bread and wine cease to exist and in their place is the true Body and Blood of Jesus Christ.

The priest is not simply telling a story and dramatizing it with gestures, as if he were taking part in a Passion Play. He is at this moment actually representing Jesus, speaking the words with authority, speaking words that have a real effect. It is like when an ambassador speaks on behalf of his nation, for instance, to make a declaration of peace; as he speaks, it actually takes effect, as if his sovereign or his whole nation were speaking through him. He does not speak as a private individual, as a news announcer simply reporting what has happened, but the words he speaks have a real and immediate effect. So it is when the priest speaks as ambassador for Christ. The words take effect as he speaks them, so that the bread becomes the true Body of Jesus as soon as the words "This is my Body" have been spoken; the wine becomes his Blood as soon as the words over the chalice have been said. That is why the Host is shown to the people before the priest proceeds to consecrate the wine.

Transubstantiation

So what is really happening? We use very simple Biblical words and say: "This is my Body; this is my Blood", but the reality behind those brief words is difficult enough to have puzzled thinkers throughout the ages. The most authoritative analysis of what is happening was provided in the thirteenth century by St. Thomas Aquinas, and the Church has made that analysis her own. Attempts have often been made to find new ways of explaining what happens at Mass, but none has been as satisfactory. The theology of *transub-stantiation* is based on an Aristotelian understanding of the way things are: that there is a difference between the inner reality of something, its *substance*, and what it seems to be, its *accidents*. What we see and taste and touch and smell of bread and wine is only accidental; the reality is what it is, the actual "breadness" that we cannot touch or taste. We can see this more clearly if we think of a person, someone we love. The real person is not just what we see and hear and touch; the real person is something deeper and more profound, so that the evidence of our senses is only superficial, not reaching to the actual substantial person.

When Jesus Christ himself at the Last Supper, or his ambassador at our daily Mass, says "This is my Body", it means that this, which still retains the accidents of bread, is actually the substance of Jesus Christ himself. It is perfectly obvious that the accidental characteristics of bread remain unchanged, and however closely you examine it with any of your senses you will perceive no difference from how it was before. What has changed is the *substance* that is imperceptible to our senses. In the same way the contents of the Chalice after the Consecration look and seem exactly the same, even to the extent that if you drink too much of it, it has the normal effect of alcohol, yet what it actually is has changed; it is the Blood of Jesus, that is to say, his Life, poured out in suffering for us.

How does this come about? It is, quite simply, through the *creative will* of God. We see in the book of Genesis that things came into being simply because God spoke a word of creation. It is by his will that everything came into being and by his will that things remain in being. For something to exist means that it is willed by God. Our own will can change the superficial meaning of something, as, for instance, when a nation decides to invest a particular combination of colors with the status of national flag. But our human will does not change the substantial nature of things; the flag is still a patchwork of colored cloth. God's will, on the other hand, is what determines the existence and nature of anything, so that when God declares that this, which looks like bread, is actually his Body, why then it really is. That is why from the moment of the Consecration we no longer refer to "bread" or "wine" except as a figure of speech; we say now "the Host", meaning the sacrificial offering, and "the Precious Blood". Together we refer to the eucharistic Species as the *Blessed Sacrament.*

Our Lord's words recall the Old Testament sacrificial language, particularly where he speaks of the Blood of the Covenant. A covenant or agreement in the pagan world was ratified with blood, which symbolized the life of the covenanting parties. Siegfried and Gunther swear friendship by drinking blood: "Blood-brotherhood will be the oath we swear. . . if a brother breaks his oath, if a friend betrays his trust, the drops that today we have solemnly drunk shall flow in rivers to propitiate a friend."[3] The Old Testament law builds on this custom and tames it; it forbids the drinking of blood but provides that it should be sprinkled on the covenanting parties. When Moses offered the great sacrifice that ratified the covenant between God and his People Israel, he sprinkled blood toward the people (Ex 24:6–8). The shedding of Christ's blood on the Cross is the reality toward which all the Old Testament sacrifices pointed. His blood falling on the earth ratified the New Covenant between God and the people of the earth, binding them together, reconciling them, "so that sins may be forgiven".

What the disciples found incredible was the invitation to eat and even more so to drink. When our Lord first began to explain the Eucharist to them, nearly five thousand people, who had been eating out of his hand, got up and walked away (Jn 6:66). The idea of eating sacrificial flesh was of course natural, indeed no meat at all was eaten without at least a vestige of the idea of sacrifice. Human sacrifice, however, was abhorrent to the Jewish people, and the invitation to "eat my flesh" incomprehensible. What he is asking, however, is not that we should devour his dead flesh, but that we should take into ourselves his living Self. In the same

[3] Richard Wagner, *Götterdämmerung*, act 1, scene 2.

way, to drink his blood means to take his true Life into ourselves. As the life of Christ cannot be divided from his self, as the body and blood of a living person cannot be separated, so we understand that Jesus is wholly present in the Host and wholly present also in the Chalice. You cannot divide him up, so we say that in either *Species* or either *kind,* of the Blessed Sacrament Jesus is present, Body and Blood, soul and divinity. That is why the priest genuflects and the concelebrants bow low in worship before the consecrated Host and again before the chalice of the Precious Blood.

The Memorial Acclamation

A curious innovation in the 1969 Missal is the *memorial acclamation.* In response to a single invitation by the priest, the people have a choice of four or five responses, which leads to difficulties in practice. The normal solution is for the priest to lead in with the first words of the response he wishes them to use, though in some parishes the number of the response will be marked up on a board. Ideally, as an acclamation, the response should be sung.

The invitation to proclaim "the mystery of faith" raises certain questions, however. The words originally come out of the formula of Consecration of the

Chalice and refer obviously to the wonder of transubstantiation and the covenant between God and his
People that is being ratified. These words now have
been moved to follow the Consecration and invite the
people's acclamation, their assent to the mystery. Yet
the first three acclamations provided seem to turn away
from the present reality and look forward to a future
coming. We seem to have an echo of the 1960s
obsession with the end of the world: the actual presence of Jesus Christ here and now on the altar is
ignored in favor of a longing for the revelation of his
glory, when he will be seen by the whole world at the
end of history. One might be forgiven for thinking
that Jesus is not here yet, that the bread and wine are
only memories of a past event, only tokens of a future
presence. But that is not the faith of the Catholic
Church, and we must understand the memorial
acclamation in accordance with that faith. Jesus really
is present; he has died and risen; he comes to us daily,
but that coming is not yet unveiled, not yet "in glory".
All the same, my own preference is whenever possible
to use the fourth acclamation, which does acclaim the
Lord in the present, and to look enviously toward the
people of Ireland, who are privileged to use St.
Thomas' words to the risen Jesus: "My Lord and my
God!"

The Anamnesis

Element (e) of the prayer is the *anamnesis,* which is simply the Greek for "commemoration". We call to mind the great events of our salvation, the death, Resurrection and Ascension of our Lord, and in that memory we offer the sacrifice. But when we say "call to mind", we must do so in the biblical sense of the words. For the people of Israel, a "memorial" or "commemoration" did not mean simply thinking about something that happened long ago; it meant reliving a past event as if then were now. The supreme example of a "memorial" is the Passover sacrifice: every year the paschal lamb was offered, and the children of Israel relived that moment of liberation by which they became a people. "This is the night" when the events are taking place, every year returning to the same moment when the Red Sea was crossed, when the People of God entered the Promised Land. The Hebrew language, unlike most European languages, does not easily talk about events as "past, present or future", and history is not seen as a single line, the arrow of time that can never turn back. Rather all time can be experienced simultaneously, every moment in history is always now. The Christian Church, too, has always kept to this way of thinking, even during the most rationalist ages when narrow minds found it incomprehensible. It was left to Albert Einstein to bring the world back to the Hebrew conception of

time and space, for a poet to express the unity of all
time and all places in a single point.

> *Here, the intersection of the timeless moment . . .*
> *The moment of the rose and the moment of the*
>   *yew-tree*
> *Are of equal duration. A people without history*
> *Is not redeemed from time, for history is a pattern*
> *Of timeless moments.*[4]

When we "call to mind" the death and Resurrection
of Jesus, we are actually making them present; that
hilltop long ago outside Jerusalem is here and now; we
are actually present at Calvary; we are now in the
garden of the Resurrection. There is only one Body of
Christ, here on this altar, and it is the same Body that
stands on every altar in every church throughout all
ages and over all the world.

The Second Epiclesis

After the anamnesis comes element (f), the offering.
Once again we call on God, offering the sacrifice in
union with all the sacrifices of the past. We ask that as
our sacrifice reaches God's altar in heaven, so we may
receive in return the eternal Gift, which is the Son of

---

[4] T. S. Eliot, "Little Gidding", in *Four Quartets*.

God. Again we must think ourselves into a Hebrew way of being; this earth is a model of heaven, and our earthly worship is in parallel to the worship of heaven. If there is an altar on earth, so there must be in heaven, and what we do here is duplicated in heaven. Now the angel is invoked to make the exchange of our earthly sacrifice for that heavenly one. The Old Testament sacrifices of Abel, Abraham, and Melchizedek are recalled, for they are "types" or foreshadowings of the Sacrifice of the Mass. Abel was the just man who accepted the will of God, the free nomad who tended his sheep like a good shepherd (Gen 4:2–4); Abraham was the patriarch who would grudge God nothing but offered his own son as a sacrifice for all (Gen 22); Melchizedek was the timeless priest-king of peace who offered bread and wine for a blessing on God's people (Gen 14: 18–20). In the second epiclesis, the miracle of transubstantiation is to be applied for our benefit. We are to receive the Body and Blood of Jesus Christ and so be filled with every grace and blessing.

Second Intercessions

The delicate structure of the Roman Canon brings us gently back to our own concerns after the high mysteries we have been contemplating. Now we pray for the dead, since we have been reassured that all time is present. Those who have "gone before us" are not, after all, remote and lost; they are with us in the presence of Christ, and we can think of them and ask that our prayers be joined with the love of God to bring them light, happiness, and peace. We pray for "all who are falling asleep in Christ", that is, for those who die at peace with God. We are one with them all in the Sacrifice of the Mass. As in the case of the commemoration of the living, the priest may be asked to make a special mention of someone departed, a *Mass intention* for the dead.

We have prayed for others; now we can pray for ourselves. Speaking on behalf of the whole congregation, the priest acknowledges our sinfulness and asks that we be forgiven beyond our deserving. In the old Mass, the words "for us sinners" was specially emphasized; even at the sublime moment of the canon of the Mass, the priest is still a weak human being, no better than the congregation he serves. Our forgiveness is asked in the name of the martyr saints, those who joined in the suffering of Christ in order to have a share in his healing love. A selection of martyrs is named, the first to shed their blood for Christ, and some of the great heroes and heroines of the Roman Church. (Again a priest in a hurry may omit many of the names.)

Final Blessing and Doxology

There follows a short blessing of "all these gifts", which it seems originally referred to the gifts brought up in the offertory procession, the fruit and vegetables, the produce and artifacts that would not only support the clergy but be distributed by the deacons to all in need. Perhaps we could refer that blessing now to the collection baskets that should be lying near the altar. By asking God's blessing on the gifts, we are asking for that blessing to extend to all for whose benefit they are used.

Lifting up the Host and the Precious Blood, the priest then sings or proclaims (h) the *doxology*, the words of praise linking Father, Son, and Holy Spirit, which bring the Roman Canon to its triumphant conclusion. The Blessed Sacrament is lifted up as a sign of achievement; the miracle has taken place; Christ is present here for us, and we unite in acclaiming that marvel with the *great Amen*, which may be sung till the windows of the church rattle.

Alternate Eucharistic Prayers

Eucharistic Prayer II

Having looked in detail at the Roman Canon, we can see more briefly how the same elements are contained in the other Eucharistic Prayers. The second Eucharistic Prayer is one of the three written during the late 1960s for the new Missal. It is based on an early text, the so-called *Apostolic Tradition* of Hippolytus.[5] Hippolytus (c. A.D. 170–236) was a controversial figure in third-century Rome, and he seems to have been a thoroughly unpleasant character, who sent most of his life in opposition to the pope and achieved sanctity only by his final repentance and martyr's death. There is hope for all of us! It is not certain actually that he is the author of the *Apostolic Tradition*, but the document is certainly evidence for third-century practice. The liturgical text stands in a tradition that continued in the East, but quite outside the Western mainstream. Our Second Eucharistic Prayer actually differs quite considerably from the original text, which lacks some of the vital elements. It is recommended for use particularly

[5] This is most easily found in Henry Bettenson, *Documents of the Christian Church* (London: Oxford Univ. Press, 1963), section VII, vi, c.

on weekdays and "special circumstances",[6] which probably means when pressure of time or a restless congregation urge the priest to speed up the Mass. It should never be used on Sundays, but occasionally when the children are very noisy and the sung Sanctus has gone on a long time some think it has to be brought out.

It begins with its own proper Preface, element (a), thanksgiving for the saving work of Jesus Christ, emphasizing the Incarnation. The acclamation (b) follows in the invariable form of the Sanctus. (Other Prefaces can be used with this Eucharistic Prayer.) Picking up the word *holy* from the acclamation, the prayer moves straight into the epiclesis (c), calling on the One who is Holy to send the Spirit to make the gifts holy. The Consecration narrative (d) follows almost in the same words as in the First Eucharistic Prayer, with the same memorial acclamation. The anamnesis (e) is very brief, recalling only the death and Resurrection of Jesus, and the second epiclesis or offering (f) is as brief, succinctly asking that we who share in Christ's Body and Blood may be brought together in unity. The intercessions (g) name the Pope and local bishop and provide an optional paragraph to mention a specific dead person before commemorating all the departed. The living and those present are barely mentioned, "have mercy on us all", but the Church is

[6] GIRM 322 b.

commemorated in union with our Lady and the apostles and saints. The final doxology (h) is made in the same words as in the other canons.

The Third Eucharistic Prayer

This prayer is a recent composition with no ancient original. It may be used with any Preface and on almost any occasion but is particularly recommended for ordinary Sundays and holy days.[7] After the Sanctus there is a further paragraph of thanksgiving, again picking up the theme of holiness and making particular mention of the formation of the Church as God's People. The epiclesis (c) is very explicit in asking the Holy Spirit to change the gifts into the Body and Blood of Jesus Christ. The narrative (d) and memorial acclamation follow as usual, but the anamnesis (e) is rather longer and makes mention not only of Christ's death, Resurrection, and Ascension but also of his coming in glory, for if all past time is made present in the eternal Now of the Mass, so also is future time. The offering (f) is most explicit, too, in asking that we, who share in the Body and Blood of Christ, may ourselves become his Body. The Church is indeed the Mystical Body of Christ, for we become what we eat, and as we feed on Christ, so we become members of

[7] GIRM 322 c.

his Body living in the world. The commemoration of the saints who are equally parts of the Church follows here, and there is provision for mentioning any saints we wish, usually the saint of the day, the patron of the church, or the founder of the religious congregation, when applicable. The intercessions (g) follow, praying for the Church, Pope, and bishop, the entire people, particularly those gathered now, and the departed. Again there is an optional paragraph to be used to commemorate a particular person. The doxology (h) follows in the invariable form.

The Fourth Eucharistic Prayer

This it appears was an afterthought and was written very quickly indeed. Since it "provides a fuller summary of the history of salvation",[8] it is meant for congregations who have a comparatively good grasp of scripture and is usually reserved for special groups, seminarians, retreatants, religious houses, and the like. In fact, it is quite appreciated by an ordinary congregation and, because it includes a prospectus of the whole sweep of Catholic doctrine, can be used as a basis for instruction (I have even tried writing a catechism for young people in the form of a commentary on this prayer).

[8] GIRM 322 d.

The Preface, which makes no mention of Jesus, only begins the element of thanksgiving (a), which continues after the acclamation (b), the usual Sanctus. This Preface is invariable, which means that the Fourth Eucharistic Prayer cannot be used on days when there is a special preface, although it may be used when there is only a seasonal one.[9] In two long paragraphs after the Sanctus, the prayer recalls the sweep of creation and salvation, all that God has done for us and all we have to thank him for. Mention of the sending of the Holy Spirit leads naturally into the epiclesis (c), which is short and succinct. The narrative (d) is slightly different from that in the other prayers, but the words of institution are the same as is the memorial acclamation. The anamnesis (e) is more developed, mentioning Christ's death, his descent among the dead, his Resurrection and Ascension, as well as his coming in glory. It flows into the second epiclesis or offering (f), in which again we are called to be the Mystical Body of Christ, ourselves to be a living sacrifice of praise. The intercession (g) as usual mentions the Pope, the bishop, and the living and the dead, and makes the interesting addition of "those whose faith is known to you alone". We pray not only for those who were Catholics during life but those who may have lived and died outside the Church but by following God according to their lights may be said to have been "baptized by desire". The

[9] GIRM 322 e.

Church is again embraced to include Our Lady and the saints, and the prayer leads up to the final doxology (h) in the usual words.

Other Eucharistic Prayers

The three Eucharistic Prayers for children and the two for reconciliation are not often used; even small children hate being talked down to, and it may be unclear when the "reconciliation" ones are appropriate. I have used them in wartime, when the Preface of the second prayer seems particularly poignant: "Enemies begin to speak to one another, those who were estranged join hands in friendship, and nations seek the way of peace together." It should not be difficult to identify the eight "elements" of a Eucharistic Prayer in each of these, as indeed in any future compositions that may be included in revised versions of the Missal.

7

Jesus Comes to Us:
Holy Communion

Priest and people together relieve the solemn tension of the Eucharistic Prayer by joining in the Our Father, the model and archetype of Christian prayer. It is customary for all to stand, and the priest invites us to pray with one of four texts, chosen according to the season or the theme of the sermon. Whether the Our Father is said or sung, all now pray it together, for it is the prayer of all God's People.

The Our Father

When the apostles asked our Lord to teach them to pray, he gave them as a model the text we call the Lord's Prayer, or *Pater Noster*. It is often the first prayer taught to the Christian child, one that we can recite from memory without hesitation. Yet it is a prayer difficult of understanding, one that needs much medi-

tation and much love to penetrate. There have been
many great commentaries on this prayer, taking it
phrase by phrase and using it as a means of instruction
in the whole of Christian spirituality. Perhaps the
greatest is that by St. Teresa of Avila in *The Way of
Perfection*, sometimes available as a separate pamphlet.
A complication for the English user is that the traditional translation of the Our Father is perhaps obscure,
particularly in the passage about trespasses. (The Scots,
translate it as "forgi'e us our debts as we forgi'e our
debtors".) By a curious irony, the version used now by
most English-speaking Catholics is that commissioned
by King Henry VIII. Modern versions have been tried
but have been very slow to catch on, largely because
the traditional version learned in infancy is so much a
part of our religious heritage, so deeply ingrained in
our subconscious, that we feel lost without it.

The Embolism

The priest picks up the last petition of the Our Father
and sings or proclaims the little prayer that rejoices in
the curious name of the *embolism*. This is an abridged
version of the ancient one, praying for deliverance
from evil and anxiety. It has been given a new twist by
introducing the idea of waiting for the coming of Jesus
Christ in words derived from St. Paul (Titus 2:13),

which could give the casual hearer the impression that Jesus is not here yet, but we are still waiting. However, the Greek text of St. Paul actually speaks not of "waiting for" but of "receiving" the object of our joyful hope; it is a present reality that we welcome at this stage of the Mass. As so often in the 1960s, translations both of St. Paul and of the liturgical text betray an obsession with the end of the world that is not authentic to the Liturgy.

The Doxology

Jesus Christ is here, and we welcome him into our lives with the doxology "the Kingdom, the power, and the glory". When this verse was inserted into the Mass, it caused some confusion over whether it should be counted as part of the Our Father or not. It has traditionally been added by Protestants. The verse actually seems to have a liturgical origin, and in the Liturgy of the Greek church it is recited by the priest immediately after the Our Father. This evidently led to its being accidentally copied into manuscripts of the Gospels: when you are writing something out by hand and you get to a bit you know by heart, you tend to stop looking at the original you are meant to be copying. As a result it was found in the late Greek manuscripts that Erasmus used for his edition of the New Testament. Erasmus' version was then used by Luther and Tyndale for their translations, and as a result the first German and English Protestant Bibles incorporated this addition. Modern scholarship, going back to the much earlier manuscripts which were unknown to Erasmus, has shown that it is not part of the original text, and so all modern versions, both Protestant and Catholic, omit the verse from the Gospels. But while it is not part of the Lord's Prayer, it is an ancient liturgical acclamation and affirms our faith in the Lordship of Jesus.

The Sign of Peace

If the insertion of the doxology caused controversy, that was nothing compared to that which surrounds the introduction of the sign of peace at this point of the Mass. The priest, following the doxology, addresses Jesus Christ directly, looking down at the Host, in a prayer citing his words at the Last Supper about peace and praying for a peace we do not deserve. We are confident in praying in the name of the "faith of the Church" while aware that the lack of peace in our world is only the natural outcome of our sins. The priest wishes that peace on all who are present, and the deacon may then invite them to exchange a sign of peace.

In the old Mass the kiss of peace was given very formally and was passed on from the priest to each person in turn among those in the sanctuary. Now it has become something of a free-for-all, as everyone in the congregation breaks out of his customary reserve and turns this way and that seeking people with whom he may shake hands. In some parishes people leave their places and wander up and down the church, searching out their particular friends or welcoming strangers. In retreat groups or on special occasions when people feel particularly close, the sign is not a formal handshake but an embrace or a real kiss. This can lead to problems, as people make for the good lookers or avoid the less favored. At school Masses the sign of peace can become something like a mass riot as bored children seize the opportunity for a little action. The Liturgy of the Mass can be held up for quite a long time until all is calm again.

Before criticizing the sign of peace, it is only fair to reflect on what the liturgists meant when they introduced it at this point in the congregational Mass. "Before they share in the same bread, the faithful implore peace and unity for the Church and for the whole human family and offer some sign of their love for one another."[1] It comes immediately before Holy Communion because that Communion is made not

---

[1] GIRM 56 b.

only with Christ but also with each other. We are going to be united in the great Sacrament that makes us one with Christ and incorporates us into his Church; therefore we show that we are united with each other. It is an act, not to celebrate existing friendships, but to heal enmities and to make new friendships. Therefore it is appropriate to exchange wishes of the peace of Christ with those next to us. Many people come to Mass with their families, and as often as not it is within the family that healing of quarrels is most needed. The stranger, on the other hand, is the one most needing to be welcomed into the congregation. I do not think the liturgists envisaged people exchanging the sign with more than just those on either side of them, and of course they had experience only of a Mass celebrated with a small number of well-behaved adults.

Why then has the sign of peace aroused so much opposition? It is one of the most frequently cited reasons why people have stopped coming to Mass, and it does seem to be the cause of great divisions. People either love it or hate it. One problem certainly is the breaking of any atmosphere of prayer and recollection; people feel that at this stage of the Mass, after the stupendous mystery of the Consecration and before the intimate touch of love in Holy Communion, we need all the help we can get to remain quiet and recollected, and the noisy irruption of the general sign of peace breaks the mood irrevocably. Others have a difficulty with greeting strangers: it is hard for the cheerful extrovert to appreciate that some people really need a space of privacy and find it very threatening when large numbers of people demand to be greeted at once. They can cope with new people one at a time, but the general melée terrifies them. (I am not talking about those with clinical agoraphobia but of a much larger number of people who are characteristically quiet and find communication difficult. They can of course be helped to overcome these anxieties, but not by bombarding them with enthusiasm.[2] The Mass should make people feel wanted, not scare them away.)

Some of the difficulties could be overcome by resituating the sign of peace. It was first moved to this point in the late Middle Ages, and for good reasons: we have just been praying for mutual forgiveness in the Our Father and are just about to communicate together. But the formal ritual of the old kiss of peace and the resulting respectful distance between persons meant that the modern difficulties did not arise. The older position for the sign was, as the Gospels suggest, after the General Intercessions and before the Offertory (Mt 5:23–24). In St. Justin's description of the Mass, this is when it takes place, and it does still on certain occasions, for instance, when a confirmation has taken

[2] See Frank Lake's *Clinical Theology* (London: Darton, Longman & Todd, 1966), in particular chap 6.

place during Mass. People are much less tense at this point, and there is already an informal atmosphere as people relax after the sermon and fumble in their pockets for the collection. Another possibility might be to have it at the very beginning, linked with the Penitential Rite. After all, if the idea is to express forgiveness and to welcome strangers, it seems odd to wait until the Mass is nearly over before noticing our neighbor. However, as I have already intimated, the penitential rite itself was originally the immediate preparation for Communion and sits rather strangely at the beginning of Mass. Moreover in most parishes many people have not arrived that early in the Mass. Yet another possibility is to have it right at the end, as the Quakers do at their meetings. That works well when a small group has been celebrating Mass and is staying together for a meal or meeting; it can help to make the transition between prayer and fellowship. Since the whole gesture is optional anyway, I believe there is scope for some future reflection, but I am far from thinking that I know of the perfect solution. In the meantime, all I can suggest is that you be sensitive to the people near you and try to greet them in a way that takes account of their personality and cultural origin. A lot can be conveyed in a smile without needing to touch the other person at all.

The Fraction

One of the most important actions of the Mass is almost totally obscured in the new rite as it also was in the old: the *fraction*, or breaking of bread. In most churches the *Agnus Dei* follows immediately after the sign of peace, which takes us right up to Communion, and people are unaware of what the priest is doing meanwhile at the altar. He takes the Host, breaks it and then drops a small portion into the chalice, accompanying the action with a silent prayer about the mingling of the Body and Blood of Jesus Christ. It is not at all clear what this is about, especially since the majority of priests then put the Host back together again and later show it to the people as if it were unbroken.

"The breaking of bread" is actually the oldest name for the Mass. Jesus took bread and broke it and gave it to His disciples, who recognized him in the breaking of bread (Lk 24:35). In the Acts of the Apostles, the only shy allusions to the Eucharist are under this title (Acts 2:42,46; 20:7, 11; 27:35; cf. 1 Cor 10:16; 11:24). "This rite is not simply functional, but is a sign that in sharing in the one bread of life which is Christ we who are many are made one body."[3] It is a natural symbol

[3] GIRM 56 c.

for two or more people to break and share some item of food together, such as an apple or a loaf of bread. By sharing in the same item, they feel united. All our problems began when two people shared an apple; all are solved when we share in the one Bread. Just as a Jewish family shares the unleavened bread, the *matzoh* at the Passover supper, so Christians break and share the one Bread which is the Body of Christ. There is an ancient prayer to accompany this action that does not appear in our liturgies: "As grain once scattered on the hillside was in this broken bread made one, so we who are many are one body, for we all share in the same bread."[4]

In practical terms, a single Host can be broken and shared only among very few. The normal large Hosts available will easily break into four, and with care into six, so that when there are only that few at Mass, all can indeed share in the one Host. It is possible to get very large hosts that can be broken into up to fifty fragments, but these produce problems with crumbs and ragged edges and have not been found really satisfactory for parish use. The result is the usual compromise of having one large Host for breaking and a great number of individual small ones for the general congregation. However the *Instruction* does expect the priest to break the large Host and "distribute [the parts] to at least some of the faithful",[5] so my own practice is

[4] Cf. *Didache,* no. 12.
[5] GIRM 283.

to break it into four and to place three of the parts in the ciborium with the small hosts. (If there is a deacon, he receives one of the fragments.)

The Commingling

In addition to the fractions of the Host intended for the priest and the people to receive, a small piece is immersed in the Precious Blood. The prayer that accompanies this speaks of the mingling of the Body and Blood of Jesus Christ, as if the two needed to be brought together. As it stands, the rite is obscure, if not downright misleading. It is very curious that this rite has survived into the new Mass, when so much that was much more obviously significant was swept away. If the Chalice is to be distributed to the faithful, there is an immediate practical difficulty, for it is not always easy for the priest to consume the particle when he drinks, and if it remains in the chalice it might be distasteful to those following after.

The meaning of this rite can only be recovered if we look at its origin, or rather its two origins. Two ancient customs are represented in the gesture, both with the same fundamental meaning. It appears that it was customary to reserve a fraction of the Host from each day's Mass and keep it until the next Mass, when it would be brought to the altar and mingled with the newly consecrated Chalice. (The subdeacon who

brought it would wait at the foot of the altar holding
it until the fraction; he retained this position of waiting, in fact, until 1964, even though the paten he held
had by then long been empty!) The idea is obvious:
today's Mass is not an isolated event, but it is one with
yesterday's and tomorrow's. All time is brought
together in this one sacrifice, and the presence of Jesus
in the Mass abides forever. The other custom was
similar, practiced at least in Rome, where the pope
would send particles of the Host from his Mass to
every church in the city so that they could be mingled
with the Blessed Sacrament in each separate church.
The Mass in each church is not isolated but is one with
every Mass being celebrated everywhere. All places are
brought together in this one sacrifice, and the presence
of Jesus is everywhere.

Hence we can see that the prayer, when it talks of
mingling the Body and Blood of Jesus, does not mean
putting together the two elements of this Mass, as if
the Host were incomplete without the Precious Blood,
but of mingling the Blessed Sacrament from previous
Masses or those in other places with what has been
consecrated here and now. The apparently meaningless
and unnoticed gesture is discovered to symbolize the
profound unity of the Mass throughout all time and
space.

The only way I can find to bring back some of the
significance of this moment in the Mass is to bring the

ciborium from the tabernacle to the altar at this point. This contains the small Hosts reserved since the previous Mass and will probably be necessary anyway to ensure that there are enough small Hosts for everyone to communicate. A fraction of the Mass Host can then be placed in the tabernacle ciborium, or one of the old Hosts transferred to the new ciborium, to make the point of unity between past, present, and future Masses. To be "authentic," one might suppose that the particle placed in the chalice should always come from the tabernacle, but the *Instruction* specifies that it should come from today's large Host.

The Agnus Dei

Whatever the priest is doing about the fraction and the commingling, the choir and people are busy with the chant "Lamb of God", the *Agnus Dei*. We remember that in the Old Testament sacrifice the lamb represented the people, whose sins would be taken away through eating it. Jesus Christ is himself the Lamb, and by sharing in his Body we are reconciled to God, and our sins are taken away. Hence the chant is appropriate at this moment in the Mass. Because the priest is occupied with the fraction, it can appear at a said Mass that the Agnus Dei is not important, since the priest starts it off and then seems to lose interest, whereas at a sung Mass it is given more prominence, often by long and elaborate settings. (Some settings are very long indeed, since they were originally intended to cover the whole period of the distribution of Communion and clearing the altar; in the new Mass it might be better to pause after the first "have mercy on us" to let the priest invite the people to Communion and then to continue while the faithful are being communicated.) While the Agnus Dei is being said or sung, the priest, having finished the fraction and commingling, has two silent prayers of preparation for Holy Communion, which are addressed to Jesus and therefore said bowed toward the Host.

Communion

The priest genuflects in adoration of the Sacred Species, straightens up, and turns toward the people to invite them to Communion. He holds up a fraction of the Host. This, he says, is the Lamb of God that you have just been invoking, this here and now is the One who takes away the sins of the world. Then yet again our attention is diverted toward the future with a quotation from the Apocalypse: What joy awaits those who are invited to the marriage supper of the Lamb (Rev 19:9). A parable used often by our Lord and taken up by St. John in the Apocalypse is the idea of heaven as a great banquet or a marriage feast. Our joining in the sacrament of Holy Communion in this life is a foretaste or token of that eternal banquet in heaven. But we have not yet been summoned to that banquet, and we may not take it for granted that we shall be.

Both priest and people then repeat the centurion's words from the Gospels, "Lord I am not good enough for you to come in under my roof" (Mt 8:8). The sensitive Roman official knew that a good Jew would not feel able to enter the home of a Gentile; he was considerate as well as humble. Our present English translation moves rather far away from the scriptural text, but the idea is still the same. We are not good enough to entertain God, but he is good enough and powerful enough to heal us by sending his Word, the Word made flesh, that is, Jesus Christ made for us into something we can eat, something we can receive under the roof of our mouths. The effect of this powerful quotation from the Gospel has been drastically reduced in the new Mass; formerly it was recited three times, first by the priest and then by the congregation. The atmosphere was built up by this repetition, bringing all to realize what a momentous event was transpiring. Now it is in danger of being swamped as the congregation begins to move in an untidy wave toward the altar.

The priest receives Communion, taking first a

fraction of the Host, then drinking from the Chalice. (If others are to receive from the Chalice, the priest tries to consume the particle of the Host that is floating in it, but this can prove frustratingly elusive!) If there is a deacon, he receives immediately after the priest. Then priest and deacon proceed to distribute Communion to the faithful.

The Communion of the Faithful

There is at present a confusing variety of methods for distributing Holy Communion to the faithful, which, like the sign of peace, can trigger strong feelings and emotions quite inappropriate to the significance of the action. The documents of Vatican II and the *Instruction of the Roman Missal* are unsatisfactorily silent on the subject. The tradition in all countries for many centuries has been that the people kneel along a step, supported by a rail or bench. The priest moves along behind the rail (usually from left to right as he sees it) and, pausing before each communicant, takes a small Host from the ciborium and places it directly on the tongue of the communicant. The latter composes himself to receive with hands joined (in some countries under a cloth lying along the rail) and the tongue brought forward to the lower lip (not sticking out as if the priest wanted to examine his tonsils). A server holds a flat metal plate or paten poised to catch the Host if it should drop or any crumbs that may fall.

The first change introduced in 1963 was to shorten the little prayer that the priest said for each communicant to "the Body of Christ" and to ask the communicant to reply "Amen". This custom seems to have been derived from the time of St. Augustine, who in one of his sermons points out that "Amen" does not only mean "Yes, I believe that this is really the Body of Christ held before me"; it also means "Yes, we, the Church, are the Mystical Body of Christ." However, having to speak immediately before receiving the Host or even as it is actually placed on the tongue is very inconvenient and often leads to the host being fumbled out of the mouth, to say nothing of disastrous collapses of false teeth.

Communion in the Hand

This circumstance added momentum to the movement that began in the mid-1960s to ask the priest to place the Host in the communicant's hands so that he could say "Amen" and receive at leisure. Unfortunately many of those proposing this change were motivated not just by the convenience of elderly parishioners with loose teeth but by inadequate and unscriptural views on what Holy Communion really meant. Rejecting our

Lord's invitation to be like little children, they asserted that it was "childish" to be fed directly into the mouth. As a result, Pope Paul VI called a referendum among all the bishops of the world to ask their views on whether Communion should be given in the hand or whether the ancient custom should be upheld. They voted 1,233 to 597 in favor of prohibiting the giving of Communion in the hand.[6] Subsequently the Pope permitted the giving of Communion in the hand unless the local bishops actively opposed it, so that now in most countries both alternatives are common. The choice seems to be left to the individual. If receiving on the hand, the approved method is to hold both hands flat, the left on top of the right. The Host is placed on the left hand; then with thumb and forefinger of the lower hand, you take up the Host and transfer it to your mouth, afterward checking carefully that there are no crumbs remaining on either hand. Naturally, clean, ungloved, unbandaged hands are expected. If you have only one hand free, encumbered for instance by a baby or a walking stick, it really is better to receive in the mouth whatever you would normally do. In practice I notice a tendency among the more serious young people to prefer to receive on the tongue, while the elderly, particularly the more intellectual, receive on the hand. In some countries fre-

[6] Austin Flannery, *Vatican Council II, The Conciliar and Post Conciliar Documents* (Newport, N.Y.: Costello, 1984) 1:151.

quent abuses have led to the bishops urging a general return to the older customs. Pope John Paul II has made no secret of the fact that he definitely prefers the old ways and often refuses to give Communion in the hand.

Communion Standing

Another change introduced over the last generation has been the custom of standing for Communion instead of kneeling. At first this meant the people standing along the step and the priest moving along as before, but this soon developed to the common modern practice whereby the people advance in a straight line toward the priest, who remains stationary. In conjunction with this, the altar rails themselves have frequently been removed. There is nothing at all in the decrees of the Council or subsequent liturgical instructions to suggest this: it is merely the fashion. Having worked for many years in parishes where both systems are used, I am now convinced that there is nothing to be said in favor of standing in line. The individual communicant is kept moving, never at rest, and has to receive Communion (whether in the hand or on the tongue) and get out of the way immediately; it all seems rather rushed. Conversely, from the priest's point of view, it is actually much slower. Moreover if (like me) he has a tendency to a backache, this is aggravated by standing in one place while swaying to and fro as people come up, now slightly to one side, now short, now tall (and there is an invariable rule that the smallest child receives on hands held low down, while the tallest adult opts for Communion on the tongue). Straightening up at the end of the rail and walking back to the beginning gets the circulation going again, so it is much less tiring, as well as quicker, to give Communion to a large congregation if everyone kneels along a rail. But as I say, the Church has made no ruling on the subject, so both methods are permissible at the discretion of the parish.

Communion under Both Kinds

Yet another innovation in some dioceses has been the general distribution of Holy Communion to the whole congregation in the form of wine as well as in that of bread, in other words, "under both kinds" or "both Species". Superficially one can be forgiven for thinking this was the original practice of the Church and wondering why it was ever not done. However, the fact remains that for the overwhelming majority of Christians throughout most of the Church's history, Communion was received only in the form of bread, and most eucharistic spirituality and devotion concentrates on the Host, the Bread of Life, from chapter 6 of St. John's Gospel onward. As I have already remarked, the Acts of the Apostles refer only to the "breaking of bread". St. Paul implies that they are alternatives (1 Cor 11:27), and the catacomb paintings depict only bread and fish (a symbol for Jesus), never wine. I think the most we can say is that in the early centuries the practice was optional, sometimes in use, sometimes not, and that as the Church grew in numbers the custom of receiving from the chalice grew ever more infrequent.

Why this should be is open to research. To a certain extent the sheer cost of wine in northern countries must have made it impossible, as it does now in parts of the Southern Hemisphere. The spread of disease, particularly the great plagues of mediæval Europe, may be a factor. A distaste for the idea of drinking blood, together with the idea that sharing in the chalice meant taking on a share in the suffering of our Lord, must have put more people off. What seems certain is that it was never a case of the wicked clergy arrogating a privilege to themselves, but rather one of the laity spontaneously declining to receive.

In any case, the mind of the Church is quite clear: we receive the whole Jesus, Body and Blood, soul and divinity under either species. You cannot divide him up or receive him only in part. To receive under both species is merely to "complete the *sign* of communion", not to add to the reality. The Second Vatican Council refused to suggest general reception under both kinds but suggested a few cases when it could be optional.[7] It became rather more widespread in only a few countries, not, curiously, those where local wine is cheap, but more often in areas where a local Protestant community survives and practices communion under both kinds. Recent scares over infection have led to it being abandoned or actively discouraged in some areas.

If Communion is offered under both kinds, there is a variety of approved methods of distribution. When there are large crowds, we have found by experiment that even if people receive the Host kneeling along a rail, only confusion arises if the deacon with the Chalice follows along the rail after the priest with the Hosts, since the majority of people do not wish to receive from the Chalice. After receiving the Host, therefore, those who wish to receive under both kinds go to a side chapel where they can receive the Chalice. It is necessary the communicant to take the Chalice firmly in both hands to drink before handing it back to the deacon, who will wipe it and turn it before offering it to the next person.

If the chalice is wiped and turned, and if it is made of non-corrosive metal (for example, gold or silver), there is said to be very little risk of infection. How-

[7] SC 55.

ever, experience shows that many diseases are transmitted by the chalice, and mouth ulcers and colds are common. This means that if you are unwell, and in particular if you have a weakened immune system and are susceptible to infection, it would be better not to approach the Chalice. You have already received the whole Christ in the form of bread. Conversely, if you are unable to cope with the gluten in bread, you may receive from the Chalice alone; again, you will have received the whole Christ; your Communion will be complete. As in the case of Communion on the hand, observation suggests that young people prefer to follow the older custom, while the elderly and the intellectuals are eager to receive from the Chalice.

Extraordinary Ministers at Communion

In many parishes, because the custom of receiving Communion standing means it takes a long time, or because Communion is to be given under both kinds, it has become usual to commission lay people to assist with giving Communion. This is another development that has caused great controversy and division, for there was no precedent before the late twentieth century for anyone other than a priest or deacon to distribute Communion at Mass. One unfortunate side effect has been that many lay people have come to believe that the role of the laity in the Church means only that they should compete with the priest for status in the sanctuary rather than carry the mission into the world. In some countries there has been confusion over the status and pastoral role of such assistants, and advice is given in the papal instruction *Christifideles Laici* (no. 23) that seems to discourage the proliferation of lay ministers with Communion. More recently the Vatican Instruction on the laity has made a more definitive ruling that lay ministers are for extraordinary occasions only, and that in no circumstances should they be habitually used.[8] How this will be applied, and how it will affect Communion in both kinds, remains to be seen.

The Sacrament of Holy Communion

In receiving Holy Communion, the reality is what we must observe and respect: this is Jesus, the Lamb of God, come to heal us, to feed us, to make us one with him. It is the completion of the Sacrifice. The priest has taken our gifts behind the veil to offer them to God, for them to be made holy. Now he returns to

[8] Congregation for the Clergy, Pontifical Council for the Laity, et al., *Instructions on certain Questions Regarding the Collaboration of the Non-ordained Faithful in the Sacred Ministry of Priests* (Vatican City, August 15, 1997), art 8.

the people bearing the sanctified Gifts so that those who receive them can themselves become holy. The priestly task is fulfilled when he distributes these gifts; the Mass is consummated when he and the faithful receive the sacrificial Lamb, the sacrament that makes us one with Christ and with each other. We become what we eat; by eating the Body of Christ, we ourselves become his Body, the Church.

8

We Bring Jesus to the World: The Dismissal

Distributing Communion to a large congregation, even with the help of several priests or deacons, can take a long time. People need some help to pray during this time and during the clearing of the altar afterward, the time when the actual action of the Mass is suspended.

The Communion Chant

A short *Communion antiphon* is supplied in the Missal for each Mass, often with an alternative. These are provided in the same way as are the entrance antiphons, and, like them, they are the survival of a responsorial psalm that was intended for this moment. The intention was that, as soon as the distribution of Communion had begun, the choir should lead the people in the singing of the psalm, with the antiphon repeated after each verse. This can indeed be done, using the same sort of psalm settings as for the other responsorial psalmody. Alternatively, the antiphon can be set to music as a motet. In practice, in most parishes an ordinary hymn is used instead. This should be chosen on the theme of Holy Communion, from the very large repertory of eucharistic hymns that exists.

It is unclear when is the best time to distribute Communion to the choir. If they are supposed to be leading the people in song, they must all be together and attending to what they are doing; even the people's part is difficult enough to sing while lining up for Communion. In large churches the common solution is for the organ to play quietly while the choir comes up first for Communion and for the antiphon or motet to begin when they are all safely gathered in. A hymn for the people may then follow, by which time the greater part of the congregation will be back in their places. At a very large celebration, it may be necessary to have more than one hymn, though there is the risk of turning it into a sing-along. It might be better to alternate choir and congregational music with organ voluntaries. The only person who really cannot receive Communion is the organist, which is why many churches are glad to employ non-Catholic organists. Ideally, I suppose, the choir and organist should attend an earlier Mass for their own devotion and to receive

Communion; their part at the high Mass can then be to aid the prayer of the faithful without forcing a conflict of interests.

The Purpose of Singing

The purpose of music or singing at Communion time is not just to entertain the troops, to keep them from getting bored while the long process of distribution drags on. Its purpose is to aid prayer, to stimulate meditation, to provide a background for contemplation. Rather lyrically, the *Instruction* suggests that the song is to "express outwardly the communicants' union in spirit by means of the unity of their voices, to give evidence of joy of heart, and to make the procession to receive Christ's body more fully an act of community."[1] As always, the authors of the *Instruction* are thinking of Mass with a small group of committed adults, and we have to face the fact that a large, mixed congregation will not be able to sing coherently while forming a tidy procession. The movement for Communion is likely to be rather ragged. Some will not leave their places until the crowd has thinned, others will leap up at once and stand for some time waiting in

[1] GIRM 56, i.

the aisles. Good singing is unlikely under the circumstances, though a well-known and popular hymn will
be taken up by all whether in their places or in the
line.

We also have to accept the fact that some are unable
to sing or do not want to. Particularly after Communion, there will be those who prefer silence and find
any sort of music a distraction. Some can return to
their places and will be happy to remain in their own
interior silence while others sing around them; others
really cannot pray against a musical background and
will probably seek out a Mass without singing. The
Church is big enough to tolerate all types!

Meditation

For those whose prayer is mostly conceptual, using
words or intellectual thoughts, the texts sung at Communion, and for that matter all through Mass, can be
a real help. If the antiphon, the motet, or hymn has
scriptural words relating to Holy Communion, they
will suggest a line of thought that turns into prayer.
They may be a reminder of the Gospel reading or
contain a theological point that nourishes our prayer.
Meditation is a form of prayer that thrives on words and
ideas, on pictures or symbols. We begin with the idea

and develop it, pondering on what it meant originally and on what it can mean for us here and now. We can reflect on our own problems and joys and how the Gospel speaks to us of them. We can, indeed we must, be aware of the others around us and their problems and joys—this is where that troublesome baby in the next pew can become part of our prayer, as we reflect on the heroic sanctity of the mother and how much she needs God's grace and our support in bringing her child to Christ.

The *General Instruction* is perhaps a trifle naive in saying that the antiphon "gives evidence of joy of heart". All too often in our fallen world, Mass must be celebrated in times of tragedy, personal or general, and our thoughts and sympathies are with people of appalling suffering. A superficial lightheartedness is just callous. Christian joy does not mean jolly music and inane smiles; it may mean weeping with those who weep, as Jesus wept over Jerusalem. It may mean sharing the intense inner wrenching pain of the bereaved, being close to those who are abandoned and lost, providing human comfort for those who feel deserted by God. We must not forget that the first Mass was celebrated in the blood and agony of Calvary. There is a joy, yes, but it is not superficial and cannot be provided at will; it comes often only through tears of pain. It is in the moment of Communion that many feel most disconsolate, and the rest of us have to be there to share and to support. This, too, is part of our meditation.

Contemplation

Others there are who cannot "meditate" in the intellectual discursive sense but whose prayer is wordless, formless, without structure. For them words and music are irrelevant and may even be a terrible distraction as they struggle to pierce the veils that hide the face of God. Alternatively, music may be a help if it simply provides a background of rhythmic noise, something soothing to blot out the abrasive sounds of the crowd moving up and down the church, the crash of chairs and kneelers and the whimpering of children. The contemplative may bury his head in his hands and let the sound of singing drift over him—it really will not help if you tap him on the shoulder and push a hymnbook into his hand!

The Antiphon Recited

If there is no choir or singing, the Communion antiphon faces the same difficulty as the entrance antiphon: it is supposed to be recited "either by the people, by some of them, or by a reader. Otherwise the priest himself says it."[2] Whenever and however it is recited, it has little impact unless you keep the text before your eyes and use it as a "point" for meditation. Reciting it as people climb out of their places to line up for Communion means that the words are lost in the clatter, and it might well be better to wait until the distribution is over and propose it then, as a theme for prayer during the silence that ensues as the altar is cleared.

The Ablutions

When Communion has been distributed, priests, deacons, and extraordinary ministers return the vessels to the altar, and there is the practical necessity of clearing up. Naturally the first concern is for the remains of the Sacred Species. The remaining small Hosts are collected into one ciborium, which is veiled and returned to the tabernacle. All attention should be on the priest who is doing this, and all in the sanctuary kneel until the doors of the tabernacle have closed, for this is Jesus Christ himself passing from our sight, just as he did at the Ascension.

If Communion has been distributed under both kinds, the Precious Blood remaining in the chalices

[2] GIRM 56, i

must be consumed. Obviously it cannot be kept in reserve, for the accidental properties of wine still remain, and those include the ability to ferment and spoil. You cannot imagine how onerous it can be to consume the remaining contents of a chalice after many people have received Communion from it, which is why most priests prefer to delegate this part to the lay extraordinary ministers. If you are the last to receive Communion, it is a real act of charity to finish the chalice before handing it back to the deacon, to spare him this ordeal.

The paten, ciborium, and chalice must then be cleansed. Tiny particles of the Sacred Host and drops of the Precious Blood remain, and these must be consumed. If the priest is saying Mass without assistants, he will collect any crumbs off the paten and brush them with his forefinger into the chalice. He may do the same with the ciborium, or he may rinse it with water and pour the water into the chalice. Traditionally, a chalice is rinsed first with wine and secondly with a mixture of wine and water, both rinsings, or *ablutions*, being drunk by the priest. This ensures that all drops are taken up and would be particularly appropriate after giving Communion under both kinds. The *Instruction* does suggest washing with wine and water but gives the alternative of water only,[3]

[3] GIRM 238.

which seems to be the common practice. Sacristans and altar servers are always very sparing with the water and may give only half a cruet to wash two ciboria and four chalices—I always like to have plenty to refresh the mouth as well as to ensure that all the vessels are properly cleaned. The vessels are dried with the *purificator*.

If there is a deacon or assistant priest, he does the ablutions, while the celebrant sits or stands aside. If Mass is being celebrated facing the people, the priest should not stand behind the altar to perform the ablutions as if the people really wanted a close look at this necessary but mundane part of the proceedings; he should stand at the side of the altar or take everything over to the side table and do the ablutions there.[4] (When Mass is said facing east, the priest will naturally be turned away from the people while washing the vessels and will not distract them while so doing.) The chalice, purificator, paten, pall, corporal, burse, and veil may be reassembled as at the beginning of Mass and either remain veiled on the altar or be taken to the side table. Other chalices and ciboria are placed on the side table, veiled if possible.

The ablutions are practical and necessary but also symbolic. They are also known as the purifications, in a curious reversal of normal usage that the Church

[4] GIRM 120, 238.

delights in. The sacred vessels have been holding the Body and Blood of our Lord; they have therefore become holy, taken out of ordinary use and made over to God, and cannot come into contact with anything secular. To bring them down to earth as it were, to make it possible to polish them, wrap them up and put them away, they must be ritually "purified". It is not that they are not pure but rather the opposite; they are too holy to touch and need to be brought into the common world again. (This is a biblical way of thinking, and very strange to us, but it is an exact parallel of the biblical concept of "purifying" a mother after childbirth: it is not that she is dirty, rather that she is so holy and has taken part in so sacred an action that she needs to be brought back down to earth before entering common life again.)

Not only the chalice but also the priest is "purified"; by drinking the cleansing water from the chalice, he purifies his mouth and makes it possible to return to daily life. Formerly all who had received Communion did the same; before returning to their places, they took a morsel of ordinary bread and a sip of unconsecrated wine as a purification. This has dropped out of use in the Western Church but is still current in the East.

Silence after Communion

While all this is going on, there should be a solemn silence in the church. Some priests prolong this by going to the chair and sitting in silence before continuing the Mass, to give everyone a chance for peaceful meditation. However, in a large, mixed congregation, this is not practicable; those who were the first to receive Communion have probably waited ten minutes or more already, and even the most angelic of small children will be restless and noisy by this stage of the Mass. Silence will return to the church only after everyone has left.

The Prayer after Communion

The priest gestures people to stand and invites them to pray. Now comes the third of the three prayers of the Mass, associated with the Opening Prayer and the Prayer over the Gifts. It will make some mention of the fact that we have just received Holy Communion and some mention of the season or feast being celebrated. It concludes "through Christ our Lord", and the congregation assents with "Amen".

Interlude: The Announcements

In nearly every parish it is necessary to make certain announcements at Mass to draw the people's attention to things they certainly will not take in from the bulletin alone. There is no ideal moment; in the past the announcements were given with the sermon, but they tended to obscure or even replace the sermon altogether. In Africa I have heard the notices being read by a layman after the priest leaves the sanctuary, but a European or North American congregation could never be persuaded to wait that long. As a result, the *Instruction* suggests they be read now after the Communion prayer, to catch the people before they get a chance to leave. Notices may be read by priest, deacon, or layperson—the only requirement is that they be audible. This is also the moment for appeals and so forth; they are not sermons and should not intrude on the time of proclaiming the Word, but can appropriately be given by clergy or lay people at this stage of the Mass. If the collection for a special appeal is taken at the end of Mass, it is doubly appropriate that appeals come here at the end, rather than before the Offertory collection, which is for the running of the local church. Naturally, if there is to be a long appeal, the people are permitted to sit for it.

The Dismissal

The Mass ends abruptly. For the last time priest and people exchange greetings, and the priest then blesses the people, who make the sign of the cross in acknowledgment. The normal form of *blessing* is very short, but there are a number of longer forms for special occasions. The one reserved for a bishop consists of four lines of dialogue, before he blesses the people by making three signs of the cross over the congregation. The *solemn blessing* begins with an invitation from the deacon to bow and pray. There are then three exhortations over the people, each one inviting the response "Amen", before the final blessing. A third form is the "Prayer over the People", which is structured as a collect, addressed to the Father, specifically asking a blessing on the gathered congregation, again after the deacon has invited them to bow in prayer.

Finally the deacon has the task of dismissing the people. The Latin text is "Ite, Missa est", which is almost untranslatable. Three English versions are provided, although generations of schoolchildren have gleefully pointed out that we reply "Thanks be to God" when told that the Mass is over and we can go. In fact the word *missa* has puzzled more than just schoolchildren. It seems to have something to do with dismissal, though in strict Classical Latin it translates as

"Go, she has been sent", which raises the question of who or what "she" is. Some think it refers to the Blessed Sacrament, which has been "sent" to those who are sick or imprisoned and cannot be present to communicate with the congregation, or that it means the particles of the Host sent from the pope's Mass to the other churches of the city to make the link between his Communion and theirs. Most commentators, however, consider that *missa* is a low Latin noun meaning "dismissal" and that the deacon is saying no more than "Go, this is the dismissal" (though we could usefully introduce the related idea of "mission" at this point). It was left for even lower Latinists to imagine he was telling them the name of the whole ceremony, and hence they called it "Missa" or "the Mass". I am not convinced that any of these explanations is right but have no further suggestions.

When Mass was to be followed by some other ceremony and the people were expected to stay, formerly they were not dismissed but warned with the invitation "Let us bless the Lord" that there was more to come. Now, if there is any following service, the dismissal is simply omitted. However, on most occasions this really is the end, and clergy and people are expected to leave with no more ado. The Missal and the *Instruction* do not provide for a final hymn, although it has become customary in most churches to sing one as the ministers leave the sanctuary. This can give them enough time to return to the sacristy, take off their vestments, and slip around the church to be able to greet the people as they emerge after finishing the hymn. If the people have to be evacuated in a hurry to make ready for the next Mass, the organist can speed them on their way with a voluntary by Messaien, or he may play Bach if there is time for them to linger in the church.

The Mass in the World

The Roman rite of Mass has always ended rather abruptly (though not quite as much as now), when we might have expected a long ceremony to give thanks for the gift of Holy Communion. But the reason for this is that the Mass does not end as people leave the church building; they carry it with them wherever they go. If we have become members of the Body of Christ, we must do the same works that he does: we go out to bring about the Kingdom of Heaven in our world, to heal the sick, cast out devils, raise the dead, and bring the good news to the poor. Every Christian has the vocation to play his proper part in the work of the Church, and the graces received at Mass provide the stimulus and the ability to carry out that vocation.

The Lay Apostolate

The Vatican II document on the Apostolate of the Laity, *Apostolicam Actuositatem*, speaks of the various forms of what used to be called *Catholic Action*, in particular, the ministry of like to like. Students are encouraged to bring the gospel to students, workers to workers, housewives to housewives. It is clear that priests and bishops cannot normally reach beyond the existing congregation. They can preach within the church, but outside, they are handicapped by their very status. Nonbelievers will not listen when a priest preaches, for, they think, he is paid to do that. But if one of their own companions, a neighbor, a work-mate, someone they meet in the golf club or the laundromat, is a believing practicing Catholic able to give a good account of his faith, that has a real impact. Not that the lay Catholic normally stands up to "preach"— he spreads the gospel far more effectively by his life, by the way he lives in the world fortified by the graces given at Mass.

A basic quadrilateral for the Lay Apostolate is *prayer and study leading to almsgiving and evangelization.* We come to Mass to hear the Word of God and have it explained to us, to receive the Body of Christ and to pray. We can extend that experience with our private prayer and study and by joining the parish in other acts of worship and in various opportunities for learning more about the faith. But all this will be sterile unless it bears fruit in almsgiving and evangelization. Perhaps the greatest tragedy in the Western Church today has been the way that lay people, while flocking to Mass, to prayer and study, seem to have forgotten the follow-up. To be an "involved" layperson does not mean simply helping in the Liturgy and attending study groups: it means being an almsgiver and evangelist. The Mass and the study group will provide nourishment for that task, but the task remains to be done.

Almsgiving means trying, in whatever way we can, to help other people in this life. For many, that vocation is perfectly fulfilled in bringing up a family, in the delicate and vital task of nurturing young Christians in human and divine virtues. For others, it is in the care of the disabled or sick members of their family. Others have no such family commitments and are able to help those who have no one else to care for them. Most parishes provide structures to help coordinate this sort of work, societies like that of St. Vincent de Paul to search out and help the needy of the neighborhood. Those overseas can be helped through well-run organizations like Aid to the Church in Need. There are many opportunities for almsgiving in every parish—though we should remember that it is not necessarily charity to throw money at the drunken beggar who lurches up to us in the street; far more beneficial is time spent helping at the local shelter or rehabilitation clinic.

Evangelization means spreading the message of Jesus

Christ to those who do not know him. Much of this we do by silent example. If the Christian mother is seen to care for her children, her husband, even her difficult mother-in-law, that in itself points people to Christ. If the Catholic parish is seen to provide assistance where it is needed, locally or overseas, that will make people think without having to publicize the work. If the Catholic home has a crucifix or a picture of our Lady hung up in a prominent place, that will attract people's attention with no word needed to be spoken. And if people do notice, if they begin to think, then they will ask questions. Usually they will begin with a silly question, but if that is well answered, they will move on to something more profound. And that is our window of opportunity to tell them about what we believe, to introduce them to the Catholic faith. Jesus hardly ever initiated a conversation; people came to him and asked him questions. If we are living the Christian life, we will not need to raise the topic of the Christian faith, for people will come and ask questions spontaneously. They will not, to begin with, come to church to hear the priest speak; they will ask the lay Catholic during the coffee break at work or in the club in the evening. If we have attended Mass regularly, we will be able to supply the answers to their questions.

Eucharistic Worship outside Mass

Meanwhile the church is never empty. Jesus Christ remains, an abiding presence, always there for us to worship. The church should be open at least for some time every day so that people can "visit the Blessed Sacrament", pop in for a few moments in the course of the day, on the way to or from work, during the lunch hour or while shopping. And to help devotion, the priest may lead various ceremonies. The most popular of these is *Benediction*, often held on Sunday afternoons. The Host is removed from the tabernacle and exhibited in a splendid holder known as a *monstrance*, set on the altar amid candles and flowers so that people can gaze at him they most love and join in hymns and prayers in his honor. The Host may be exposed for a few minutes or for one hour (a *Holy Hour*) or for a longer period, classically for *forty hours,* when priests and parishioners take turns in praying continually for the needs of the Church and the world. The actual Benediction is a blessing given at the end of the period of exposition, when the priest lifts the monstrance and with it makes the sign of the cross over the people, to the accompaniment of bells and incense. In a few churches, though the number is increasing, the Blessed Sacrament is exposed perpetually, so that at any time people can come in to pray in the sight of their Risen Lord. A busy city-center church will have someone praying in it almost all the time.

Holy Communion is also taken from the tabernacle to those who cannot come to Mass. It is one of the special duties and privileges of the priest to visit the sick and the imprisoned and to bring them Communion. In every parish there will be some who are confined to their homes, and the visit of the priest is their main contact with the Church at large. A small Host is carried in a metal container, a *pyx*, taken straight from the church to the sickbed; the priest "salutes no one on the road, and his first words on entering the house are 'Peace be to this house'" (Lk 10:4–5). The little ceremony of giving Communion is adaptable to the age and health of the sick person. The priest's presence in the sickroom is vital, but lay members of the congregation should naturally be visiting as well, to comfort and assist the sick and to prepare them for the sacraments. If a priest is really unable to visit, it is possible for a commissioned lay minister to being Communion to the sick or housebound, though too often this has been an excuse for the priest himself never to visit the sick. It is difficult to know what else he could be doing that is more important. The recent Instruction on the laity stresses this point—and also reminds us that only the priest can validly hear the confession and anoint the sick person.[5]

---

[5] Congregation for the Clergy, Pontifical Council for the Laity, et al., *Instructions on certain Questions Regarding the Collaboration of the Non-ordained faithful in the Sacred Ministry of Priests* (Vatican City, August 15, 1997), art 9.

The deacon may tell us that the Mass is over, but in reality it never ends. At every moment the Mass is being celebrated somewhere around the globe; continuously Jesus Christ is coming into the world, to sanctify his people, to feed them with his Body and Blood, to build them up to be his Body, the Church. The Blessed Sacrament remains in the tabernacle as the heart of every parish, the center from which flow all our works of almsgiving and evangelization. The people, who form the Church, are dispersed throughout the unbelieving world to bring Christ's presence to all they meet, to leaven the mass of humanity so that all shall rise together. The Church is the living presence of God on this earth, the *Sacramentum Mundi*. It is through the Mass that the whole world is to be saved.

9

Appendix: The Latin Mass

When the Second Vatican Council was called, only three questions were really in everyone's mind about the Church. These were: What are we going to do about Communism? What can the Church say about artificial contraception? Should the Mass be celebrated in modern languages? The first two questions were not on the Council's agenda (the first one has answered itself), but the third one was discussed, and the result was that "the use of the Latin language (except for special cases) should be retained in the Latin rites."[1]

What the Council Said

The statement that Mass in Latin is to be in Latin sounds like a tautology, until we work out what the Council means, putting together the apparently contra-

[1] SC 36, 1.

dictory paragraphs 36 and 54 of the Constitution on the Liturgy. It would appear that the intention of the bishops was that Latin should be the normal language of the Mass, but that, particularly in non-European countries, the parts said aloud could be in modern languages provided that everyone is able to join in—and also that everyone should be capable of joining in the Mass in Latin when necessary. It was never the intention of the General Council that Latin should be totally abolished or should become an exotic rarity. The fact that it has disappeared is due to other factors still unexplained.

When the new Mass was promulgated in 1969, it was ordered that Missals printed in modern languages should contain the Latin texts as well, which the English ones do. The *General Instruction* defends the use of modern languages on the curious grounds that "no Catholic would now deny the lawfulness and efficacy of a sacred rite celebrated in Latin."[2] In effect, however, a very large number of Catholics do deny that Latin has any place in the modern world, and for many the question is considered to be closed; whatever the Council meant, Latin is now dead and should be buried.

[2] GIRM, introduction, 12.

Why Do People Want Latin?

Not all those who like Latin are able to say why they like it, and for those brought up in an exclusively modern Church, it seems inexplicable. If the Mass is so boring in English, it must be much worse in a dead language. What is the point of praying in a language you don't understand? How can the Mass possibly be valid if no one knows what it means?

To explain why so many people find that they do prefer the Mass in Latin, we need to look briefly at what worship is and how prayer works. If we examine the teaching of St. Thomas Aquinas, and of more modern writers such as Evelyn Underhill or Dom John Chapman, O.S.B., we can discern something of how God communicates to the human soul, how we can be aware of the presence of God. Worship that remains purely at the level of the human intellect is not really prayer; it is simply an exercise in mutual admiration and exhortation. Worship, to be genuine, must lift us out of ourselves and direct us toward God, who is incomprehensible and indescribable. Forms of words and actions are only symbols that we human beings can use to help us raise our hearts and minds to the transcendent. Briefly, prayer is a matter of the heart, not merely the head.

We may use the head during prayer, just as we use hands and voices, but the real business of prayer is at a much deeper level of our being. You can call it the "unconscious" in modern terms, the "apex" or "base" of the soul, in St. Francis de Sales' phrase, or just use the biblical word "heart"; there is an important part of ourselves that is not accessible to the conscious intellect but that is the seat of our deepest feelings, the focus of our love, the point where we can communicate with God and he with us. It is very rare for God to communicate through our senses; not many people hear voices or see visions, but in our unconscious heart God speaks to us all. When we use words in prayer, they are only a preparation, a vehicle, a means by which God can speak to us. After all, we can tell him nothing he does not already know far more profoundly than we know it ourselves.

Contemplation

There are traditionally three types of prayer: vocal prayer, meditation, and contemplation. Vocal prayer seems to remain mainly in the head; we talk to God just as we talk to other people. Meditation, the speciality of the Jesuits, is an exercise of the intellect in which one thinks carefully and profoundly about the things of God. Contemplation is a purely wordless prayer. We open our hearts to God, are aware of his presence and of our longing for his love, but there are no conscious intellectual thoughts. The surface of the mind is idle: everything is going on at a deeper level, in the "heart" or the "apex of the soul". Words mean very little; they glance lightly off the surface. An unfortunate by-product of this form of prayer is that, since the conscious mind is not occupied, it will flit happily about among irrelevant or even irreverent thoughts, which can be as irritating as flies in the summer. People get very worried about these "distractions", but really they do not matter at all and should simply be ignored. The real business of prayer is going on in the depths, and it is a waste of time to come back to the surface just to concentrate on banishing distractions. For the contemplative soul, it is actually impossible to keep the attention on the intellectual surface of the mind and still be able to pray. If the natural contemplative is forced to remain at the level of vocal prayer, he will be unhappy and frustrated, will not, in fact, feel he has been praying at all. This is what happens when contemplatives are faced with the new Mass in their own language: it is an agony to them because, in order to keep in touch with the words, they are blocked from praying. When they do find a Latin Mass, particularly if a great part of it is silent, they feel much more relaxed and will remark that "that really felt like going to Mass again." But most people, not having read St. Thomas or Abbot Chapman, do not understand why they feel like that, and since they have been told they ought to like the new Mass in English, they actually feel ashamed and guilty at having enjoyed the experience of Mass in Latin.

The experience of many years hearing confessions has convinced me that a very large proportion of people, much larger than most Jesuits would admit, are naturally contemplatives but do not know it. The more intellectual and educated people are, the more likely they are to live in the rational, conscious mind and prefer vocal or intellectual prayer. It is children and the less articulate, people who can communicate directly with God in contemplation. But because they are less articulate they cannot defend their own position, and the intellectuals have succeeded in making them feel inadequate. This explains the curious fact that people who understand Latin are the most likely to defend the liturgical changes and prefer Mass in English, while those who do not understand Latin are often the ones who love the Latin Mass and most regret its abolition. And of the younger people, born since the changes, it is the uneducated poor who are most likely to react spontaneously in favor of the Latin Mass if by any chance they stray into one.

Pray As You Can and Not As You Can't

Abbot Chapman was insistent that we each need to find our own mode of prayer and develop that, without trying to pray in a way that does not suit us. We cannot say that one form of prayer is "better" than another or be envious of other people because they pray in a "higher" mode; the right way for me is the best and highest way for me. Acceptance that other people are different is the first step toward a harmonious resolution of the problem of Liturgy that has split the Church. If you are an intellectual and can pray happily using the vernacular words of the new Mass, do respect the contemplative soul who feels happier with a Mass that he "feels" rather than "thinks". The Latin Mass can be experienced on many different levels, for the educated intellectual is capable of following the words and keeping them in mind; the Jesuit can pick up a "point" from some part of the text and meditate against the background of words and music while the simple contemplative can open his heart to God, aware of the great action of the Mass, the coming of Christ to his people, but oblivious to the actual words.

Attention to the Words

The most frequent worry I hear in confession is that of people who feel anxious and guilty because they cannot keep their minds on the literal meaning of every word during Mass. They imagine they are being willfully inattentive and are missing out on what the Mass is all about. I do not think many of them believe me when I tell them that almost everyone (including priests) has this experience and that in fact I believe it to be absolutely impossible to pay attention to every word that is spoken during Mass. Moreover, I believe it would be undesirable to do so. The theory under which the liturgical experts restructured the Mass was indeed that every word should count and that the people should remain on the level of intellectual understanding throughout. I do not believe that even liturgists can do this, though they probably feel they ought to. For the majority of people, prayer just does not work like that. They may, if they are of the more intellectual, meditative type, pick up a few words, the punch line of one of the readings, or just a sentence from the Eucharistic Prayer and make that the subject of a formal meditation. If they are more contemplative, they may well find that none of the words of the Mass touches the surface of the mind but that as soon as they begin to pray they become indifferent to the torrent of words. If the Mass is in English and they are expected to get up and down and join in the words frequently, they will feel instinctively that this is an interruption to their prayer. When Mass is in Latin (or in any language other than their own), it is much easier to rest in a formless, contemplative sort of prayer, where the mind has little to do and the heart is open to God.

What I have said may be rather controversial, but it is based not only on what I have read but on the expressed feelings of many people of all levels of intelligence and all walks of life. So many have told me that they cannot attend to the sense of the Mass; so many have anxiously confessed to being distracted during Mass, unable to fix their minds on the words, and so many have claimed to find relief from these worries when they find a Mass in Latin that I am not prepared to brush them aside as fanatics or cranks. I believe that there are different ways of experiencing God in prayer and that people have a right to the form of worship that helps them.

Pope John Paul II

I feel on safe ground in saying this when I reflect that the present Pope has made it very clear that he shares these views. In words that must be unprecedented on the lips of a modern pope, he has actually apologized for the extraordinary way in which the changes of the

Mass were carried out without sensitivity to the feelings of the faithful or any consultation of the simple laity who were the most bewildered: "I would like to ask forgiveness—in my own name and in the name of all of you, venerable and dear Brothers in the Episcopate—for everything which, for whatever reason, through whatever human weakness, impatience or negligence, and also through the at times partial, one-sided and erroneous application of the directives of the Second Vatican Council, may have caused scandal and disturbance concerning the interpretation of the doctrine and the veneration due to this great Sacrament."[3] He goes on to urge charity and mutual respect in "drawing from the rich treasure of Revelation things both new and old". The Holy Father has made it quite clear, on numerous occasions, that he would like to see the Mass celebrated in Latin, in the old form, as a regular and easily available alternative to modern languages and that, by providing for those who prefer Latin as well as those who are happy with modern languages, he hopes to bring to an end the divisions within the Church that so hamper our missionary work.

[3] Pope John Paul II, 1980 letter to the bishops on Holy Thursday, quoted in Austin Flannery, *Vatican Council II, More Post-Conciliar Documents* (Northpoint, New York: Costello, 1982), 2:85.

An International Language

A totally different consideration, and one that should be obvious, is that there is a real need in the modern world for an international language that does not carry political implications with it. When people of many different languages are gathered, as happens more and more frequently now, it may be a practical expedient to use one of the dominant world languages, French, English, or Spanish, but it is unjust to the people who speak minority tongues. Latin has the advantage that no race or political system can claim it as its own; it belongs to the world. The old Polish doctor, whom I mentioned earlier, in the prisoner-of-war camp was able to accept the German military chaplain as a priest not only because of his vestments but more significantly because he celebrated Mass in Latin. Had the Mass been in German, the last vestige of familiar home comfort would have been taken away. Another experience that has influenced me was my visit to an off-shore island now ruled by a neighboring great power. The people have their own language, but that language was prohibited in public life, in schools, and also in the Mass. In the Latin days, they used to sing Latin words to their own native music and felt at home with it; now they had Mass in the mainland language and could sing only hymns and music imported from the mainland. The Mass itself became an instrument of the government in suppressing local culture. In a world full of refugees and oppressed peoples as well as a world of migrant workers and even tourists, the abo- lition of an existing international language seems no- thing short of absurdity. It is not quite too late to repair the damage.

The Church's Treasury of Music

Another consideration that is not unrelated to the present interest in Latin is the existence of an enor- mous "treasury" of sacred music, nearly all of which was written for Latin words. The Council was insistent that this "treasure must be retained and valued, and that choirs should be carefully promoted, especially in cathedral churches".[4] Of course there is a great heritage of English church music, though most of it was written for Anglican services such as Evensong and does not easily find a place in the Mass. Modern composers are doing their best to supply the gap, but with all due respect to them, we have not since 1969 had time yet to produce a repertory in English to compare with the compositions of Palestrina, Monteverdi, Haydn, or Mozart. Moreover, the ancient music of the Church, Gregorian chant, is becoming increasingly popular. Concerts and recordings of Latin church music are always in demand, and the few churches that follow

[4] SC 114.

the Council's instructions and promote a choir capable of performing the great composers are sure of an enthusiastic congregation.

The musical heritage that was composed for Latin simply cannot be abolished because fashions briefly changed. Nor can most compositions easily be put to English words; Latin is a language full of vowels and hardly ever ends a word on a double consonant. English is more consonantal. I remember sitting through a responsorial psalm once that a well-meaning composer had set to an old Gregorian melody: it involved the congregation spluttering out the word "hosts" at the end of every response. Again it is the experience of ordinary people that listening to a well-trained choir singing Latin polyphony can help them to pray in a way that joining in a simple English hymn does not. This may be precisely because the words are unintelligible. No matter how well you know Latin, you cannot follow the words of some Haydn Masses any more than you can follow all the words of an ensemble by Puccini or a finale by Gilbert and Sullivan. It is the overall effect that lifts up the soul and shapes its moods. The compassionate sympathy of a Requiem or the soaring exultation of an Alleluia can speak to the soul who is quite unaware of the literal meaning of the words used. Many people prefer not to sing themselves; they would much rather remain silent while great music wells around them, letting it be the background and accompaniment of their contemplative prayer. The naive insistence that every member of the congregation must join in fails to take account of the reality and complexity of human nature.[5]

Old Rite, New Rite

When most people talk about the "Latin Mass", they tend to mean instinctively the old form of Mass as it is remembered from before 1962. There is a popular belief that this form of Mass has been prohibited and that it is disloyal and even immoral to want it back. As a result, many conscientious Catholics are ashamed of feeling any nostalgia for the old days and would not dare attend a Mass in Latin, even in the new form. I have said enough to show that it was never the intention of the Council or Pope Paul VI to prohibit Latin; indeed, the new Mass is officially promulgated in Latin and may be celebrated in that language by any priest whenever he feels it appropriate. There is no disloyalty whatsoever in celebrating in Latin when it is the clearly expressed wish of the present Pope, all his predecessors, and the very Council itself. Yet when visitors stumble upon the English Oratory churches and attend

---

[5] A brilliant discourse on the present state of Church music is Thomas Day's *Why Catholics Can't Sing* (New York: Crossroads, 1990).

Mass in Latin, their reaction is usually one of guilty delight, as if they have happened on something nice but naughty.

The use of the old form of Mass is a different issue. It was certainly the intention of the liturgists to prohibit any future use of the old Missal, but Pope Paul VI refrained from prohibiting it and, in certain cases, granted explicit permission for it to continue. The present Pope has gone much farther in urging that it should be restored and made freely available for those who request it, ordering all bishops to "make generous provision" for those who are unhappy with the new Mass and would like the freedom to worship in the way their ancestors did.[6] Unaccountably, many bishops have failed to implement this papal decree, although increasingly it is now possible to find churches where the Mass is celebrated regularly in the old rite in Latin. The difficulty has arisen because certain groups use the old rite as a figurehead for rather dubious doctrines, reviving the old heresy of Jansenism, which concentrates on the fear of God and denies his compassionate love for all men. In some countries, this old-rite Jansenism is also heavily involved in politics of an unsuitable brand. A touchstone of orthodoxy in this particular controversy is devotion to the Sacred Heart of Jesus. This concept, linked to the practice of frequent Holy Communion, was encouraged in the

[6] Pope John Paul II, apostolic letter *Ecclesia Dei*, July 2, 1988.

seventeenth century to emphasize the human love of the God made man for us in opposition to the harshness of Jansenism. Still today devotion to the Sacred Heart serves to distinguish the true "traditionalists", who simply want to pray the Mass in a way that suits them, from the politicized sects who use the old Mass as a recruiting gimmick.

In English-speaking countries, the political and unorthodox groups have made little headway, but the old rite is still rare because of an Anglo-Saxon respect for law and order; people tend to want to be obedient to what they think authority requires. As long as most Catholics believe the pope has banned the Latin Mass, they will be suspicious of it, whether in the new rite or the old. I hope what I have said will help to clear the air a little.

The Eastern Rites

I have from time to time mentioned the Eastern rites when their liturgical practice serves to illuminate something in the West. Historically these developed in the Eastern Empire of Constantinople and territories to the east and south of that. As those regions became more and more isolated from Rome and the West, so their liturgical traditions developed on different lines, until the form of Mass in the East became very different from that in western Europe. The spread of Islam and the destruction of the Empire fragmented Eastern Christianity, and in certain areas, notably Ethiopia, the Church developed alone with very little contact with other cultures. There are several different actual rites and families of rites, nearly all of which exist both in and out of communion with Rome. The tragic separation of the Eastern Orthodox Churches from Rome and the West came about for all the wrong reasons, and that separation persists still for political and nationalist reasons, not for anything profoundly theological. The Eastern Churches in communion with Rome (most of whom dislike being called "uniate") preserve exactly the same liturgical traditions as their contemporaries outside the Roman communion, so that a Russian or Greek Catholic Mass will appear identical to the equivalent Orthodox Liturgy.

Most Eastern Catholics living in traditionally Western countries follow the Liturgy of St. John Chrysostom—the most familiar in Britain and North America are the Ukrainian communities. The Liturgy may be celebrated in any language, Greek, Old Slavonic, modern Ukrainian, or even English, but the ceremonies and the chants remain the same. There is much use of harmony, and often different voices will sing different words at the same time. The choir may be in full flood when the deacon or priest appears and sings loudly over the top of them. To attempt to follow the text will be futile; every word has a meaning, but it is the totality, the whole effect of music, color, light, and scent, that speaks to the soul. The technique is to let yourself be immersed in the all-round experience and allow the Liturgy to lift your heart, not so much your mind, to God. In comparison to the great Eastern Liturgies, the most elaborate polyphonic Latin Mass seems transparent and intellectual.

The Once and Future Mass

Whatever form of Mass you celebrate, whether it is in the full splendor of imperial Russia or in a simple English classroom, it is the same thing that is happening. Whatever varieties of language, movement, and music, the same eternal action is taking place. This is the sacrifice of Jesus Christ; through this, Christ comes again to us, and in this we are caught up into his Body, the Church. Any form of the Western Mass will follow the same structure; you can discern the opening rites, the act of penance, the Gloria, the Collect, Liturgy of the Word, Creed, Offertory, Preface and Eucharistic Prayer, Communion, and Dismissal. Once you know what is happening at Mass, you should be able to know what is going on, no matter what language is being used. When on holiday in Hungary or Honolulu, you can attend Mass in the local church and know that you are one with that congregation as with every other Catholic congregation in the world. If you are in Beirut or L'viv, you can still join the local Eastern Catholic church in worship, though you may need to look more carefully to know when the various parts of the Mass come.

The Mass is the Mass, wherever and however it is celebrated. Naturally you will find some forms of Mass more congenial than others, just as you will find some priests easier to deal with than others. You have a right to search out the celebration where you are most happy, but other people have that right as well. If you travel out of your home parish to find your favorite church, you have no right to despise those whom you meet going the other way to Mass in the church you have just left. And if you cannot avoid attending Mass in a style you dislike, remember that it is the one, eternal Mass, and no matter how uncongenial the surroundings, how boring the sermon, how fatuous the priest, it is the Sacrifice that matters. Christ has come to earth for us, come let us adore him!

Index